Nintendo

Originally founded in 1889 as a manufacturer of playing cards, this book examines the history and political economic status of the multinational consumer electronics and video game giant Nintendo.

This book offers a deeper examination into Nintendo as a global media giant, with some of the industry's best-selling consoles and most recognizable intellectual property including Mario, Pokémon, and Zelda. Drawing upon the theory of the political economy of communication, which seeks to understand how communication and media serve as key mechanisms of economic and political power, Randy Nichols examines how Nintendo has maintained its dominance in the global video game industry and how it has used its position to shape that industry. This book argues that while the company's key figures and main franchises are important, Nintendo's impact as a company – and what we can learn from its evolution – is instructive beyond the video game industry.

This book is perfect for students and scholars of media and cultural industries, critical political economy of media, production studies, and games studies.

Randy Nichols is Associate Professor in the Division of Culture, Arts & Communication in the School of Interdisciplinary Arts & Sciences at the University of Washington Tacoma. His work focuses on the critical political economy of video games. He has published three books: *The Video Game Business* (2014), *Inside the Video Game Industry* (2016), and *Political Economy of Media Industries* (2019), as well as various articles and book chapters analyzing the interplay of the video game industry with other media industries and the implications of video games on cultural and creative industries policy.

Global Media Giants
Series editors
Benjamin J. Birkinbine, Rodrigo Gomez and Janet Wasko

Since the second half of the 20th century, the significance of media corporate power has been increasing in different and complex ways around the world; the power of these companies in political, symbolic and economic terms has been a global issue and concern. In the 21st century, understanding media corporations is essential to understanding the political, economic and socio-cultural dimensions of our contemporary societies.

The **Global Media Giants** series continues the work that began in the series editors' book *Global Media Giants*, providing detailed examinations of the largest and most powerful media corporations in the world.

Vivendi
A Key Player in Global Entertainment and Media
Philippe Bouquillion

Alibaba
Infrastructuring Global China
Hong Shen

Bertelsmann
A Transnational Media Service Giant
Mandy Tröger and Jörg Becker

Baidu
Geopolitical Dynamics of the Internet in China
ShinJoung Yeo

Nintendo
Playing with Power
Randy Nichols

For more information about this series, please visit: https://www.routledge.com/Global-Media-Giants/book-series/GMG

Nintendo
Playing with Power

Randy Nichols

R Routledge
Taylor & Francis Group

NEW YORK AND LONDON

First published 2024
by Routledge
605 Third Avenue, New York, NY 10158

and by Routledge
4 Park Square, Milton Park, Abingdon, Oxon, OX14 4RN

Routledge is an imprint of the Taylor & Francis Group, an informa business

ISBN: 978-0-367-46909-2 (hbk)
ISBN: 978-0-367-77640-4 (pbk)
ISBN: 978-1-003-03191-8 (ebk)

DOI: 10.4324/9781003031918

Typeset in Times New Roman
by Apex CoVantage, LLC

This book is dedicated to my parents.

Contents

Figures

Tables

Acknowledgments

This project felt the full impact of the pandemic, complete with multiple family illnesses and hospitalizations, personal injuries, loss of travel and access, changing teaching modalities, somehow more meetings and e-mails rather than less, not to mention general malaise. As such, this book would not be possible with the extreme patience of series editors Benjamin Birkinbine, Rodrigo Gomez Garcia, and Janet Wasko as well as the gracious folks at Routledge. In addition, a whole series of writing groups and friends-as-editors have created spaces to work, offered invaluable feedback and encouragement, and their own insights and questions about Nintendo as a company, so thanks in no particular order to Chris Demaske, Andrea Modarres, Pamela Krayenbuhl, Emma Rose, Alexandra Nutter, Ed Chamberlain, Riki Thompson, and Bill Kunz. Finally, I want to express my gratitude for the funding and support from the University of Washington Royalty Research Fund.

1   Introduction

For an entire generation, the name Nintendo is synonymous with video games. Nintendo's best-known brands can be found licensed across a range of media. Those same brands have been both the subject of intense fan devotion and fertile ground for emulation and piracy on a global scale. And yet, to include Nintendo in a series titled Global Media Giants might seem a surprising choice, given how it differs from how many of the other companies' media scholars typically discuss in this category. Unlike some of the longest standing global media giants like Disney, Newscorp, and Bertelsmann A.G., it is a company focused on a single industry. And unlike some of the newer entries into the list of global giants like Alphabet, Facebook, and Tencent, Nintendo's fortunes are not so reliant on data generation and Internet technologies. In fact, it is not even the biggest company in the industry it does focus on – video games – where it competes with Sony, Microsoft, Electronic Arts, and Tencent among others. Still, Nintendo belongs squarely among those giants, having earned its place there because of how it has bucked a number of industry trends and established others, allowing the company to successfully navigate both the rapidly growing global video game industry and to continue to adapt and thrive. Nintendo grew from a small family business focused on the manufacturing of playing cards founded at the end of the 19th century to being an industry leader in one of the fastest growing and most profitable entertainment industries at the start of the 21st century.

Tracking the history and development of Nintendo as a business provides an excellent primer on the development of the global video game industry. One of the company's most famous advertising slogans, from which this book derives part of its name, is "Now you're playing with power" (Koch, 2016). That slogan provides a central conception not just to how the company needs consumers to feel about its products, but also about where and how the company itself sees its key advantages. Nintendo has rarely pushed beyond games, emphasizing that it is a company focused on play and fun. But it has never seen these things as necessities to its audiences. As a company, many of the challenges it has faced from its first video game on are challenges the entire industry has struggled with. Since the first video game companies emerged in the 1970s,

DOI: 10.4324/9781003031918-1

the industry has reinvented itself a number of times. As it has changed, game franchises – names like *Pac-Man, SimCity, Doom*, and many others – have come and gone. So, too, have the companies that developed them. And trends in the industry and how we play video games have changed as well: from arcades to personal computers to consoles and handhelds, and, finally, on mobile phones. That said, many of the company's decisions have run counter to its competitors, particularly those grounded in other industries. As such, Nintendo offers both lessons and cautions in the political economy of games and in the larger firmament of global media industries.

Founded in 1889, the company manufactured playing cards, moved into arcade game manufacture in the 1950s, and began exploring game development in the 1970s and 1980s (Nintendo, 2008; Sheff, 1993). Nintendo's entrance into the video game industry is often credited with saving the industry, which had been in a downward spiral (Provenzo, 1991; Sheff, 1993). By way of example, Nintendo's first products hit the U.S. market in 1986, and by 1990, its hardware and games accounted for approximately 90 percent of the U.S. games market (Nichols, 2014). The company's entrance to the video game industry was marked by tight control of both hardware and software production, intensive control of their intellectual property (IP) and its licensing, and focus on key demographics tied to particular hardware platforms. Of particular note was the company's rigid control over software development, a tendency which has resulted in repeated litigation even as it has been central to the company's longevity and success.

From its earliest days, a majority of Nintendo games were developed by external companies who signed licensing deals. However, the company stipulated that any game must be developed subject to Nintendo's specifications and final approval while the developer had to shoulder the cost of development and cartridge manufacturing in addition to agreeing not to develop for competing companies (Moffat, 1990). Perhaps the best example of the company's success has been its continued dominance in the hardware sector. The company's game consoles, which include 1983's NES system to 2017's Switch have been viable in each generation of hardware they've competed in, even as competitors like Sega have fallen to the wayside and new challengers like Sony and Microsoft have come to the fore. This is particularly impressive as a number of industry analysts have suggested that the games industry can only support two consoles at a time (Pereira, 2002). While that point is debatable, the video game industry has functioned as an oligopoly since the 1980s. Companies like Sega and Atari have come and gone in that period. Nintendo, however, has not only been a consistent industry leader as well as one that has had tremendous impact on the other companies in the industry. More impressively, the company has been number one in the handheld market since the introduction of the original GameBoy in 1989. Perhaps most crucially, Nintendo has resisted what Wesley and Barczak (2010) call "the performance trap," the tendency by high-tech industries to emphasize ever increasing technological prowess as a way to drive continued consumption. One example of this for the video game industry has been an emphasis on increasing graphical complexity and realism, trends Nintendo has been much more conservative about adopting.

This book argues that Nintendo needs to be understood beyond the typical framing of a company making toys and entertainment for children. Rather it is one of a number of dominant media companies in the world, and it has reached this status not just through business strategy but by developing connections to other transnational companies and through the support of a variety of State actors. The central focus of this project is an examination of how Nintendo has maintained its dominance in an otherwise volatile industry. Nintendo's strategies and inner dealings have largely been a mystery. This project aims to pull back that veil to look at how the company has used its power to maintain its success. Like all of my work, it draws on the critical political economy of communication, which seeks to understand how communication and media serve as key mechanisms of economic and political power. Because video games represent what Kline et al. (2003) call "an ideal commodity" for understanding high-tech and cultural industries in the 21st century, an in-depth examination of the company and its practices is needed. In order to do this, it is necessary to understand both how video games are made and what their role is when we consume them.

Because of the company's longevity and success in a volatile industry as well as the cultural reach of many of its products including the GameBoy, Mario Bros., and many others, Nintendo is an ideal case study for understanding this. While there have been a number of examinations of Nintendo in its decades-long history, most of these have focused on either particular franchises or key figures (see Ryan, 2011), the importance of particular platforms (see Sloan, 2011; Altice, 2015), or about particular historical moments such as the company's arrival in America or its battles with rival Sega (see Sheff, 1993; Harris, 2014, respectively). Most of these histories have ignored the company's role and focused on either the technologies or the cultural impacts. Those elements are certainly important to the company to be touched. However, this project seeks to address the black box that is Nintendo as a company and how the company is organized and connected to create those technologies and have those cultural impacts. Doing so allows us to understand not just its history but the company's role in the present-day global video game industry.

What Is the Global Video Game Industry?

Simply put, the global video game industry consists of all the firms involved in distributing and using resources needed to make video game products, all the products those firms produce, all the labor required to produce those products, all the resources used in that labor, and, of course, all the choices about what to do with those products. That involves a range of production sectors including hardware manufacturing, software development, software publishing, retail and distribution, marketing, licensing, quality control, and many others (Ruggill et al., 2016). And, of course, it involves consumers – video game players – who consume the full range of products the industry produces. Video game production is spread out globally as is consumption, though far from equally in either case (Nichols, 2013).

The industry itself is volatile; its structure – the way resources are distributed, polices are made, and labor is divided up among other things – has changed over time (Nichols, 2014). The modern industry has developed a relatively stable structure consisting of sectors of hardware manufacturing, software development, software publishing, and retail (Williams, 2002). And in turn, that has meant that a relatively stable number of key firms of which Nintendo is one has also developed. Currently the industry functions as an oligopoly, dominated by a very small number of firms. But changes in how any one of those sectors function – such as the development of digital distribution or to the audiences who enjoy games or the policies which govern the industry – can result in new players emerging, old players falling to the wayside, or the industry restructuring itself in response (Nichols, 2014).

As an example, consider how where video games are played has altered the industry. As Carly Kocurek (2015) discussed, arcades provided a particular (and often problematic) function not only in how video games were used but also in how the industry operated. For more than a decade, arcades were the primary space for game play. In part, that owed to the size and cost of the machines themselves, but it also relied on – and shaped – a series of social conventions. As both the machines themselves and the social conventions around video game play shifted, the industry had to as well. Video game play moved from arcades to our homes. Video game play became mobile. When that happened, companies like Atari and Activision saw their fortunes shift. Some companies left the industry entirely. Others thrived. Nintendo was present during those shifts and thrived when they happened. But why?

Overview of the Book

The goal of this book, then, is twofold: first, to understand Nintendo's role in the global video game industry and what we might learn from it; second, via that understanding, to demonstrate Nintendo's impact and importance as a global media giant. It is hoped that through both of these goals, something might be learned that is applicable beyond our understanding of video games to other media industries. But to do so, this book draws on a critical political economic framework, seeking to understand Nintendo both historically and in terms of its power relations within the industry.

One of the common refrains that resists studying companies like Nintendo or products like video games is that they're just entertainment. But a critical political economic framework recognizes that a company like Nintendo and its products are important for a variety of reasons beyond the simple issue of whether we enjoy ourselves. In the production of its products, Nintendo makes choices about and influences how other companies and individuals use scarce resources. In providing content for entertainment, both the company and its products help to shape our understanding of the world as well as our own use of time and other precious resources. Critical political economy recognizes that there is a consequence to what we make, what we purchase, and what we enjoy. The subsequent chapters are designed to help understand some of those consequences.

Chapter 2 begins by providing a detailed history of Nintendo from its origins in the 19th century through 2020, focusing on the development of the company itself and its key decisions and products along the way. It divides the history of the company into three primary eras: the company's founding through to approximately the 1960s; the 1960s through the 1980s, when it began to focus on toys and electronic games; the 1980s through the mid-1990s, when the company was establishing itself as a pillar of the video game industry; and the mid-1990s through 2020, when the company truly exercised its power as a global media giant. Over the course of that history, many of the patterns and practices discussed in Chapters 3–5 are established.

Chapter 3 examines the company's economic profile, drawing on historical patterns. Like the rest of the industry, Nintendo has centered around console cycles, releasing new consoles roughly every three to five years. But more so than most other companies in the industry because of its narrow focus, it has operated with much thinner margins. With this in mind, the chapter examines the company's two primary markets – hardware and software – in order to better understand the role each of them plays in the company's success. It, then, looks at the company's use of licensing and outsourcing, its patterns of IP control, maintenance of cash reserves, and minimizing of component costs as key strategies in navigating those margins. Next, it examines how the company is structured to facilitated relationships with key production partners and related industries. It concludes by looking at the company's recent moves toward integration and expansion beyond video games.

Chapter 4 draws on both the history and the company's strategies around IP to look at the ways the company wields its power culturally and politically. It provides a deeper look at how a range of Nintendo brands have been used historically across other media, including film, television, and print. Next, it provides an overview of the range of litigation Nintendo has been involved in, centering this is one of the key ways the company has engaged politically. This examination focuses on four key areas: antitrust, copyright and piracy, patent and competition, and consumer lawsuits. These areas draw on examples of a range of litigation dealing with emulation, fan creations and purchases, virtual trespass, and Read Only Memory (ROM) sites. The chapter concludes by looking at Nintendo's attempts to address criticisms about questionable environmental practices.

Chapter 5 draws together the key ideas and issues previously raised, to provide both an overview of how best to think about the company of Nintendo and its role as a global media giant. It begins by looking at some of the results of the company's successes in the era of the Nintendo Switch and resulting from Nintendo's first moves toward integration. It then considers the company's role in the modern video game industry and at the pivotal role IP plays in the company's success globally. Finally, it offers some key areas of concern for the company going forward and provides jumping off points for further research.

References

Altice, N. (2015). *I am error: The Nintendo family computer/entertainment system platform.* Cambridge, Massachusetts : The MIT Press.

Harris, B. J. (2014). *Console Wars: Sega, Nintendo, and the Battle that Defined a Generation* (1st ed.). New York, NY: It Books, An Imprint of HarperCollins Publishers.

Kline, S., Dyer-Witheford, N., & De Peuter, G. (2003). An Ideal Commodity? The Interactive Game in Post-Fordist/Postmodern/Promotional Capital. In *Digital Play: The Interaction of Technology, Culture, and Meaning* (pp. 60–78). Montreal: McGill-Queen's University Press.

Koch, C. (2016, July 21). Nintendo Brings Back Retro "Now You're Playing with Power" Slogan for New NES Classic Edition Ad. *Tech Times.* https://www.techtimes.com/articles/170917/20160721/nintendo-brings-back-retro-now-youre-playing-with-power-slogan-for-new-nes-classic-edition-ad.htm

Kocurek, C. A. (2015). *Coin-Operated Americans.* Minnesota: University of Minnesota Press.

Moffat, S. (1990, November 5). Can Nintendo Keep Winning? *Fortune, 122,* 131–132, 136.

Nichols, R. (2013). Who Plays, Who Pays? Mapping Video Game Production and Consumption Globally. In N. B. Huntemann & B. Aslinger (Eds.), *Gaming Globally: Production, Play and Place* (pp. 19–39). New York: Palgrave MacMillan.

Nichols, R. (2014). *The Video Game Business (International Screen Industries).* New York, NY: Palgrave Macmillan on Behalf of the British Film Institute.

Nintendo. (2008). *Company History.* Nintendo, Ltd. http://www.nintendo.com/corp/history.jsp

Pereira, J. (2002, April 19). Showdown in Mario Land – Game Makers Create Deluge of Titles as Microsoft Makes It a Three-Way Race. *Wall Street Journal,* A13.

Provenzo, E. F. Jr. (1991). *Video Kids: Making Sense of Nintendo.* Cambridge, MA: Harvard University Press.

Ruggill, J., McAllister, K., Nichols, R., & Kaufman, R. (2016). *Inside the Video Game Industry.* London: Taylor & Francis Group.

Ryan, J. (2011). *Super Mario: How Nintendo Conquered America.* New York: Portfolio Penguin.

Sheff, D. (1993). *Game Over: How Nintendo Zapped an American Industry, Captured Your Dollars, and Enslaved Your Children.* New York, NY: Random House.

Sloan, D. (2011). *Playing to Wiin: Nintendo and the Video Game Industry's Greatest Comeback.* Singapore: Wiley Asia.

Wesley, D., & Barczak, G. (2010). *Innovation and Marketing in the Video Game Industry: Avoiding the Performance Trap.* Farnham, Surrey, England; Burlington, VT: Gower; Ashgate.

Williams, D. (2002). Structure and Competition in the U.S. Home Video Game Industry. *JMM – The International Journal on Media Management, 4*(1), 41–54.

2   The History of Nintendo

The history of Nintendo is, in a sense, the history of the video game industry itself. The company was a presence in all the major eras of the industry,
having emerged as a dominant force in the 1980s and never ceding its status
through the next four decades. But the company's history goes back much
further and is illustrative of a range of trends, both in terms of how we think
about video games, the industry that makes them, and a larger trajectory of
media industries. Perhaps most crucially, the company has also been willing
to buck industry trends at key moments, which has proved instrumental in its
longevity.

Key to the company's success has been its willingness to partner with and
learn from established companies, to wait for favorable conditions and insist
on favorable contracts, and to seek control of its supply chain – particularly
distribution – whenever possible. Many of these tendencies can be seen long
before the company became the multinational, global 21st century firm discussed in subsequent chapters.

Early History

The company that would become Nintendo began as a manufacturer of traditional Japanese playing cards called hanafuda in 1889 Kyoto (Nintendo
History, 2021). Founded by Fusajiro Yamauchi, an artist and craftsman, the
company was then called Marufuku Company, Ltd., and would continue to be
run by members of the family well into the 21st century (Ashcraft, 2011; Rene
et al., 2014; Sheff, 1993). Table 2.1 details the heads of the Nintendo company
in all its incarnations since its founding through 2020, as well as their tenure
and any familial relation to the company's founder.

In 1886, the Meiji era government eased roughly 250 years of restrictions
on card games, provided the cards used pictures rather than numbers (Ashcraft,
2011; Sloan, 2011). Founded in a part of Kyoto that was, at the time, dominated by yakuza, Japanese organized crime, the company's products found an
easy home with groups of gamblers that frequented the area (Ashcraft, 2011).
Hanafuda cards were traditionally manufactured from birch bark, making them

DOI: 10.4324/9781003031918-2

Table 2.1 Historic Corporate Heads and Leaders of Nintendo and Its Major Groups

Name	Years Served	Relation to Founder	Title
Nintendo LLC.			
Fusajiro Yamauchi	1889–1929	Founder	Founder and President
Sekiryo Yamauchi	1929–1949	Son-in-law	President
Hiroshi Yamauchi	1949–2002	Great grandson	President
Satoru Iwata	2002–2015	No relation	President
Tatsumi Kimishima	2015–2018	No relation	President
Shuntaro Furukawa	2018–Present	No relation	President
Nintendo of America			
Minoru Arakawa	1980–2002	No relation	President of Nintendo of America
Tatsumi KImishima	2002–2006	No relation	President of Nintendo of America
Reggie Fils-Aime	2006–2019	No relation	President of Nintendo of America
Doug Bowser	2019–	No relation	President of Nintendo of America
Nintendo of Europe			
Satoru Shibata	1990–2018	No relation	President of Nintendo of Europe
Stephan Bole	2018–	No relation	President of Nintendo of Europe
Koji Miyake	2018–	No relation	CEO/Chairman of Nintendo of Europe
Nintendo of Korea			
Hiroyuki Fukuda	2006–	No relation	President of Nintendo of Korea

Source: (Nintendo Wiki, 2023a, 2023b, 2023c, 2023d, 2023e, 2023f, 2023g, 2023h; Sloan, 2011)

thicker than Western playing cards, and were painted with 12 suits, one for each month of the year, to create a 48-card deck. The company called its cards Daitoryo (translated to "president") and were, for a number of years, the most popular in Kyoto (Sheff, 1993).

When sales of the Daitoryo line began to taper, Fusajiro began to manufacture a cheaper line that he called "Tengu," which was both the name of a Japanese mythical character and a symbol for both playing cards and gambling (Ashcraft, 2011). Nintendo has typically been translated to mean "leave luck to heaven," though there are alternate translations including "deep in the mind we do what we have to do" and "work hard but in the end it is in heaven's hands" (Sheff, 1993). The true meaning is ambiguous; even descendants of the company's founder aren't sure of the exact meaning of the name. But at least one alternate translation suggests Nintendo could mean "the company allowed to sell hanufada," a sort of sly advertisement for the gambling usage of the company's products. Others have suggested that the "Nin" portion of the company's name suggests its own connections to organized crime in the 19th and early 20th centuries (Ashcraft, 2011). Business did so well, particularly when gambling parlors began to open, that Yamauchi began to hire apprentices to assist their manufacturer and created a sort of mass production system for the cards (Sheff, 1993).

This success of the various lines of hanufada combined with the increasing presence of Western influence in Japan led to Yamauchi manufacturing Western style playing cards beginning in 1902, though other sources indicate this happened in 1907 (Nintendo History, 2021; Sheff, 1993). These cards were first manufactured for prisoners during the Russo-Japanese War, but sales quickly expanded (Rene et al., 2014). To help with distribution, Yamauchi negotiated with the Japan Tobacco and Salt Public Corporation to expand his distribution beyond his own shops. This was a particularly good arrangement as Japan Tobacco and Salt Corporation held a monopoly at the time (Sheff, 1993). Having solidified its place in the Japanese market, by 1925, the company began to export hanufada cards to Korea, Australia, and even South America (Rene et al., 2014). By the time of Yamauchi's retirement in 1929, the company was the most profitable playing card company in Japan (Sheff, 1993).

When Fusajiro Yamauchi retired, he had no direct male heirs, and so his son-in-law took over both the company's management and his father-in-law's surname (Sloan, 2011). Sekiryo Kaneda became Sekiryo Yamauchi, leader of the largest card manufacturer in Japan (Sutherland, 2012). In 1933, he established a joint-venture company, renaming it Yamauchi-Nintendo, to help with distribution and to expand its Western playing card market beyond Japan. He also relocated the company from its original two-story building to a new space constructed next door (Sheff, 1993). Leading up to and during the war, Nintendo struggled like many companies but eventually rebounded in part due to its contract to supply cards to U.S. troops. In this period, the company's products were squarely aimed at adults, with products such as nude playing cards (Ashcraft, 2011). As the company continued to grow, it needed better control of its distribution, and so, in 1947, Sekiryo founded Marufuku Company Limited. During his tenure, the company also adopted assembly lines and a rigid managerial structure in which managers competed with each other over performance, who were noted for being particularly tough on their subordinates (Sheff, 1993).

In 1949, following a stroke the year before, Sekiryo Yamauchi turned over the reign of the company to his grandson, Hiroshi, who was only 21 at the time (Harris, 2014; Sheff, 1993; Sutherland, 2012). As part of his taking control of the company, Hiroshi Yamauchi asked that a cousin also working for the company be let go to make it clear who was in charge and he dismissed all of the company officers who had served under his grandfather (Pollack, 1996). It was Hiroshi Yamauchi who had the desire to expand the company's reach, in terms of both what industries it competed in and, particularly, in markets beyond Japan. And in 1951, under his leadership, the company changed its name to

Nintendo Playing Card Limited (or Nintendo Karuta), moving it a step closer to becoming the company we know today (Nintendo History, 2021). According to Sloan (2011), this move was designed to both signal the company's main area of business and help it ink deals with American firms.

The company continued its lines of adult themed products, including a card deck featuring Marilyn Monroe's centerfold images from *Playboy* (Ashcraft, 2011). But Hiroshi Yamauchi had bigger goals: product differentiation and, eventually, globalization. The first steps taken were consolidation, particularly its manufacturing facilities in Kyoto (Nintendo History, 2021). Next, he began attempts to expand the company's interests, venturing into taxis, noodle soups, and love motels among other ventures (Ashcraft, 2011; Sheff, 1993). The company also attempted a toy similar to LEGO's, and it was sued over the likeness though it won on a technicality (Ashcraft, 2011). Perhaps most crucially, the company began to secure licensing rights, securing a deal with Disney to manufacture playing cards featuring Disney (Sheff, 1993). Sales of the Disney card decks would exceed 600,000 a year, proving both lucrative and an important lesson for the future (Sloan, 2011). But it wasn't the company's only foray into licensing Western characters. In the 1960s, the company, working as part of a consortium with the University of Kyoto and Omikenshi company, manufactured a line of ramen noodles featuring King Feature's character Popeye; there was even a special promotion offering consumers of the ramen a chance to win a pack of *Popeye* playing cards (Popeye Ramen, 2019). *Popeye* would later feature heavily in the formative stages of one of the company's first major video game successes, *Donkey Kong* (Ryan, 2011).

Toys and Electronic Games

By the early 1960s, the company was ready to begin its expansion. It began by opening a Tokyo branch in 1961, and in 1962, it was first listed on both the Kyoto Stock Exchange and on the second branch of the Osaka Securities Exchange. Within a year, the company would change its name to Nintendo Co, Ltd, its current name (Nintendo History, 2021). But one of its key developments happened by chance. The company's president was visiting one of its factories, where he encountered an engineer, Gumpei Yokoi, hired in 1965 to maintain hanafuda manufacturing machines. Yokoi had built a toy for himself, an extending hand, and Yamauchi was so taken with it, that he ordered development of it by the company with the hope to be sold at Christmas. The product, "the Ultra Hand," sold more than 1.2 million units during its first holiday season in 1966, marking the start of Nintendo's move into toys and games (Ryan, 2011; Sheff, 1993).

Yokoi, an electrical engineer, began to experiment with electronic toys, leading to some of the company's other big successes including the popular baseball batting toy, the Ultra Machine, released in 1967; the Love Tester, released in 1969; the Ten Billion Barrel Puzzle, released in 1980; and even an early remote-controlled vacuum cleaner called the Chiritorie,[1] and it was out of this department that the company would eventually begin its foray into video games a few years later (Sheff, 1993; Sloan, 2011). The move into toys was significant for Nintendo because it not only marked a shift in their target audience but it also allowed them to begin thinking more earnestly about its global presence, at a time when Japan itself was beginning to make inroads globally, often by producing goods more cheaply and quickly than other, more established businesses in the West (McKevitt, 2017).

Yamauchi went a step further, establishing an R&D department in the early 1970s, focused on games under Yokoi's direction, hoping to continue its successes (Sloan, 2011). By 1982, the R&D department had approximately 20 employees with Yokoi as the manager, and they were tasked with developing electronic toys for Nintendo (Iwata Asks, 2010). It is worth noting that within the study of video games, a distinction is drawn between electronic games and video games. This distinction typically relies on the specifics of the parts used – video games use microchips, like computers (and so are also frequently called computer games), while electronic games are more likely to rely on older technologies (DeMaria, 2003; Mayra, 2008). At the time Nintendo's R&D group was beginning its exploration of electronic games, the first video game company – Atari – was being founded in the United States, and its first video game – *Pong* – was released, earning the company millions (Cohen, 1984). Some of the first products developed by this new department were the company's 1970 *Beam Gun*, the 1973 game that built on Beam Gun technology and simulated skeet shooting called *Laser Clay Shooting System* that was popular in bars. Many of the company's experiments in electronic gaming were less successful. Among those were *Wild Gunman*, horse racing game *EVR Racing* (Ryan, 2011). But the company was gaining valuable insight into what worked and what didn't in arcades, and this knowledge would be vital in helping vault the company's status in the 1980s. But it was the 1977 launch of the TV Game 6 and TV Game 15 consoles that were some of the first moves by the company toward making what we think of as video games (Nintendo History, 2021). This effectively made Nintendo an early pioneer in the games industry, helping to create first-generation consoles even before the company began to work developing arcade games, which is often what is credited as its entry into the industry.

Both the Beam Gun and the TV Game 6 and TV Game 15 were created in partnership with other major Japanese companies. The Beam Gun was made and distributed in Japan in partnership with Magnavox, while TV Game 6 and TV Game 15 were developed in partnership with Mitsubishi Electric (Sloan, 2011). This allowed Nintendo to study the issues related to high-tech manufacturing before starting to tackle it formally on its own. As part of the process, Yamauchi insisted that the company develop the consoles with a lower production cost than its competitors and more quickly. The Beam Gun sold for between 4,000 and 5,000 yen, and sold more than 1 million units. Both TV

Game 6 and TV Game 15 made comparable sales, making both highly profit-able for the company (Sheff, 1993). This decision helped make those early consoles succeed even as it marked a vital strategy in many of Nintendo's later successes.

Yokoi's next success was built around the idea that games might be able to be run on watch batteries. Essentially the forerunner to all of the handheld and mobile games of today, Nintendo was experimenting with the combination of electronics and video games, and the result was the company's Game & Watch series, the first of which was a simple game titled Ball, released in 1980 (Ryan, 2011). The Game & Watch series used liquid-crystal display (LCD) for its games, the games worked until the batteries ran out and, most notably, fea-tured Nintendo's D-pad, a cross-shaped controller still used in video games today. The company would release roughly a total of 60 Game & Watch games before retiring the series (Sloan, 2011). Games in the series were also color coded – for example, *Ball Silver* or *Ball Gold* (Ryan, 2011). This color coding pattern should be familiar to anyone familiar with Nintendo's later Pokémon series of games.

Based on all of these experiences, Nintendo began to shift its business from both the manufacturing of cards as well as toys and electronics to video games. This meant adjusting to a range of industry segments – hardware manufactur-ing for both arcades and home consoles, software development and publishing, and distribution. This also meant thinking about markets beyond Japan at a time when many were beginning to write the video game industry off as a dan-ger, a fad, or both (Nichols, 2014).

Becoming Global via Video Games

Just as Nintendo was moving more formally into video games, the global games industry itself was imploding. The most drastic example of this was Atari, which, in 1980, was beginning to experience the struggles that would result in its fall from dominance just a few years later. Much of this difficulty owed to issues of control over the supply chain, particularly of software development and cartridge manufacturing (Nichols, 2014). Recognizing these challenges, Nintendo began to shore up its own production practices, starting with build-ing its own factory in the city of Uji, in Kyoto Prefecture (Sloan, 2011). That same year, the company made its first move to establish a more international presence, creating Nintendo of America in New York City (Ryan, 2011). One of the challenges the early industry faced was the relationship between hardware manufacturers and software publishers. Throughout much of the 1970s and into the 1980s, there was little formal relationship between the two segments of the industry. This meant that it was relatively easy for developers to put rushed and often poorly tested software into the market, but hardware manufacturers received the blame (Nichols, 2014). Part of why Nintendo has been credited with helping to revive the industry was its response to this challenge. It would also begin to use highly restrictive software development agreements with outside developers that left much of the cost with developers while most of the profit went to Nintendo (Nichols, 2014; Sloan, 2011).

By 1980, Nintendo was ready for more, and so founded its subsidiary Nintendo of America in April of 1980 (Sheff, 1993). Initially housed in New York City, to be closer to the center of U.S. toy manufacturing, Nintendo of America quickly moved to Redmond, Washington, putting it closer to much of what would become the U.S. high-tech manufacturing on the West Coast. In short order, the company began to work on its distribution channels, starting by putting two truck drivers who had been importing Nintendo consoles into the United States as its first distributors, working on commission (Ryan, 2011). The company was initially led by Minoru Arakawa, Hiroshi Yamauchi's son-in-law, and began with only six people on staff (Ryan, 2011; Sloan, 2011).

Nintendo already had considerable experience manufacturing arcade games for the Japanese market. Many of these were thinly veiled remakes of more successful games launched by other companies, sometimes on other platforms. In the early 1980s, a successful game like *Pong*, *Pac-Man*, or *Space Invaders* might inspire a range of rip-offs across platforms and in arcades, and this posed a problem for the industry (Sheff, 1993). The first arcade game Nintendo attempted to place in U.S. market followed this trend. Titled *Radar Scope*, it was a game inspired by the success of *Space Invaders*, and though it had performed adequately in Japan, it was a failure in the United States (Ryan, 2011). The game itself didn't do well, and because of the cost and time involved in manufacturing – Nintendo was still manufacturing the games in Japan and shipping them to the United States – another solution was sought. Nintendo's solution was twofold. First, to speed the company's entrance into the U.S. market, Nintendo of America began to presell its game cabinets to arcade owners as a way to minimize the impact of construction and shipping time (Ryan, 2011). Second, the company created conversion kits that would allow existing arcade cabinets to be updated to new games. At that time, a new arcade machine cost approximately U.S. $2,500; Nintendo's conversion kits would allow arcade owners to update to a new game for roughly U.S. $800 (Harmetz, 1984). The hope was that the company's next game would be enough of a success to make up for the losses incurred (Ryan, 2011). The replacement game was 1981's *Donkey Kong*, and it would mark one of the key successes of the company, one which it would continue to profit from for decades.

Designed by a young designer, Shigeru Miyamoto, under the oversight of Gumpei Yokoi, *Donkey Kong* was originally intended to be a game featuring King Features' character Popeye (DeWinter, 2015; Ryan, 2011). However, because the company was unable to secure the license, the game itself was adapted, with the lead character initially being named Jumpman but later changed to Mario. Donkey Kong would go on to spawn multiple franchises and the original game itself would be one of the best-selling arcade games of

Table 2.2 Best-Selling Arcade Games of All Time

Game Title and Year of Release	Manufacturer	Units Sold	Estimated Revenue (inflation adjusted)
Pac-Man (1980)	Namco	400,000	$7,681,491,635
Space Invaders (1978)	Taito	360,000	$6,612,228,000
Street Fighter II (1991)	Capcom	200,000	$3,582,553,228
Ms. Pac-Man (1982)	Midway	125,000	$2,494,552,816
NBA Jam (1993)	Midway	20,000	$1,704,501,968
Defender (1981)	Williams Electronics	60,000	$1,588,463,873
Asteroids (1979)	Atari	100,000	$1,346,548,823
Mortal Kombat II (1993)	Midway	27,000	$787,607,559
Mortal Kombat (1992)	Midway	24,000	$748,462,000
Donkey Kong (1981)	Nintendo	132,000	$686,262,000

Source: ("Report: Top 10. . .," 2015; International Arcade Museum, 2023)

all time (Steinberg, 2017). Table 2.2 details the best-selling arcade games of all time, noting their manufacturer, year of release, and number of units sold. Three of those games were made by Nintendo, and all three carry connections to *Donkey Kong* itself. The game would prove to be integral to many of the company's successes and came at a particularly crucial time. Released first in Japan, then in the United States, and finally in Europe, by 1982, Nintendo was manufacturing 50–100 units daily and had begun work on a U.S. factory that would be able to make 250 more units daily. In fact, Nintendo had declined offers from a number of U.S. manufacturers to produce its games, in part because it viewed previous contracts between Japanese companies and U.S. manufacturers as particularly unfavorable ("Japanese TV Game . . .," 1982).

The game was named one of the hottest products of 1982 in the United States by Sales and Marketing Management magazine, producing approximately $200 million in sales and licensing revenue ("And the Winner..," 1983). *Donkey Kong* was so successful, in fact, that cheap attempts at copies being made across the border in Canada led to Nintendo and other arcade console manufacturers, own suit (Helwing, 1983). Its popularity also resulted in drawing the attention of Universal City Studios, which sued Nintendo over alleged copyright violations of King Kong; the suit was ultimately dismissed by the U.S. Court of Appeals for the Second Circuit ("Nintendo/Universal . . .," 1984). That success helped the company create its own sales network in the United States, bringing together 80 wholesalers around the country by 1982 to help it get its products into arcades ("Japanese TV Game . . .," 1982). The success of the game gave Nintendo entry into the U.S. home video game market as well. And it brought the company other partners. In 1982, toy giant Parker Bros. paid what was the largest advance royalty for any arcade game for the Nintendo-created *Popeye* arcade game. The advance was said to be roughly $2 million with an additional $4 for each console cartridge sold. At

that point a console game cartridge cost approximately $6 to be manufactured but might sell for between $25 and $40, giving Nintendo a handsome cut (Harmetz, 1983).
This was crucial because the arcade market was in decline. In 1982, coin-operated games were making $8 billion; that number shrunk to $5 billion by 1983 (Harmetz, 1984). Perhaps most crucially, it allowed the company a window into the U.S. home console market. Console manufacturer Coleco licensed Donkey Kong for its Colecovision system, including a copy of the game with every console sold, earning Nintendo $5 million in royalties in 1983 (Harmetz, 1983). Coleco's license with Nintendo was a selling point for investors and buyers of the company, especially when combined with an additional licensing deal with Universal City Studios ("Coleco's New Video . . .," 1982). But *Donkey Kong* wasn't enough to save the Colecovision, which entered a challenging market at a downturn. By 1982, the U.S. home video game market had peaked, and it would continue to contract until 1988 ("Nintendo to Sell Video Game . . .," 1985). So severe was the collapse of the U.S. industry that the company that had dominated it for almost a decade, Atari, was forced to pull out of Japan in 1984, only a year after it had established a subsidiary there ("Atari Inc.," 1984). This was particularly ironic as Atari had, in 1983, signed a licensing deal with Nintendo, to produce games and content for worldwide distribution based on Donkey Kong, Donkey Kong Jr., and Mario ("American Firm . . .," 1982; "Atari Signs . . .," 1983). But the crash took down more than just Atari; it drove toy industry giant Mattel out of the video game industry while companies like Bally and Activision took serious financial hits that would take them years to recover from (Kocurek, 2015). In a few years, Atari would be a cautionary tale to the video game industry while Nintendo would begin its reign as one of the industry's oligopolistic powers.

Global Dominance

By the early 1980s, Nintendo was beginning to operate globally, with exports to Europe, Southeast Asia, and elsewhere projected to reach 15 billion yen by the end of 1982 ("Video Games Will Be Made . . .," 1981). By early 1982, the company has sold approximately 2.5 million units of the Game & Watch, and Donkey Kong was still taking off. The success of the Game & Watch and *Donkey Kong* spurred Nintendo's growth. Based largely on those two properties, the company's net profits were estimated to grow by nearly 3 percent in 1982 ("Nintendo's Profit Zooms . . .," 1982). At that point, the company was so successful that it was top among 807 Japanese companies surveyed based on its consolidated earnings per revenue share ("Matsushita Electric . . .," 1983). Among the company's major investors at the time were a number of major banks including Kyoto Bank, Daiwa Bank, Sanwa Bank, and Tokai Banks ("Nintendo to Sell 1.5 Million . . .," 1983). And the company continued to work with partners. That same year, they developed a television incorporating an 8-bit microprocessor, the same type common in the first generation of consoles, with Sharp ("Sharp Develops . . .," 1983). At that point the company was selling just over 1 million units in Japan, which gave it 45 percent control of the Japanese games market. That was considerably smaller than the 17 million units being sold in the United States, but Nintendo was undaunted ("Sales of Video Games . . .," 1984).

Just as the company's success was taking off, the global market for arcade games was in rapid decline. True, there were successful games. The recently launched *Ms. Pac-Man* had sold more than 100,000 units in 1984, making it the best-selling arcade game in history through that year (Harmetz, 1984). But the writing was on the wall, and Nintendo would need to find a new product. That product was the Nintendo Family Computer, or Famicom, launched in Japan in July 1983. The Famicom was the company's first true video game console, and the first of many. Table 2.3 details all of the consoles released by Nintendo, their year of release, years of support, and what console generations they represent. The Famicom sold for approximately 15,000 yen or roughly $100 at its introduction. That price was about half the cost of competing console systems at the time and was close to cost, meaning Nintendo wouldn't make much on the consoles; instead, the company would have to make its money on games (Sheff, 1993). It was a gamble that succeeded. Sales of video games topped 1 million units in 1983, and Nintendo was producing 500,000 units of the Famicom, which still left them unable to meet demand ("Sales of Video Game . . .," 1984). The console came with three games, ported versions of *Donkey Kong*, *Donkey Kong Jr.*, and *Popeye* (Kent, 2001; Sloan, 2011). And despite a disaster with the first round of chips that resulted in a product recall and reissue, the game was a huge success (Kent, 2001). By 1984, the company had signed rival developer Namco and Hudosn Soft Co. to develop games for the system in addition to what Nintendo would create. Those developers had to pay a 10 percent fee to develop for the platform, and Hudson Soft agreed to an additional 20 percent fee because it couldn't make its own cartridges, a rate that would still be in play within the games industry decades later (Mochizuki and Savov, 2020). The Famicom was so successful that in 1985, Nintendo's profits jumped by 20 percent, to roughly $146 million, even as the company's arcade game sales were in sharp decline ("Nintendo's Recurring . . .," 1985).

Nintendo had global aspirations, and the Famicom marked its path forward. After the game's success in Japan, Yamauchi decided it might have global appeal (Sloan, 2011). The next stop would be to take the console to the United States where, like the arcade market, the console market was in decline (Nichols, 2014). Nintendo invested in a $3 million advertising campaign to run from October to December 1985 in order to launch the rebranded Nintendo Entertainment System (NES) in the United States ("Nintendo to Sell Video Game . . .," 1985). Game systems in the United States were selling for between $200 and $350 at the time, but the NES was priced at $100, and the company hoped to sell as many as 200,000 units ("Nintendo to Sell Video Game . . .," 1985; Sheff,

Table 2.3 List of Nintendo Platforms

Name of Platform	Year of Release	Type of Platform	Years Supported	Lifetime Sales in Millions of Units	Hardware Generation
Famicom/Nintendo Entertainment System (NES)	*Famicom:* Japan, 1983 *NES:* North America, 1985 Europe, 1986 United Kingdom, 1987	Console	1983–2003	61.91	Third
GameBoy	Japan and North America, 1989 Europe, 1990	Handheld	1989–2003	118.69	Fourth
Super Famicom/Super Nintendo Entertainment System (SNES)	*Super Famicom:* Japan, 1990 *SNES:* North America, 1991 Europe, 1992	Console	1990–2003	49.10	Fourth
Virtual Boy	Japan and North America, 1995	Console	1995–1996	0.77	Fifth
Nintendo 64	Japan and North America, 1996 Europe, 1997	Console	1996–2002	32.93	Fifth
Game Boy Advance	2001	Handheld	2001–2008	81.51	Sixth
GameCube	Japan and North America, 2001 Europe, 2002	Console	2001–2007	21.74	Sixth
DS	Japan and North America, 2004 Europe, 2005	Handheld	2004–2013	154.02	Seventh
Wii	2006	Console	2006–2017	10.23	Seventh
3DS	2011	Handheld	2011–2023	75.94	Eighth
Wii U	2012	Console	2012–	13.56	Eighth
Switch	2017	Handheld	2017–	124.6	Eighth

Source: (Welsh, 2017; VGChartz.com, 2023; Nichols, 2014; VGLegacy, 2023; Jurkovich, 2020; Nintendo, 2023)

1993). Sales would initially start in New York in 1985 and would expand to the rest of the United States by 1986. At the time of its release, 14 games were available ("Nintendo to Sell Video Game . . .," 1985). By 1987, the NES was the number one toy in the United States and its game, developed by Miyamoto, *The Legend of Zelda* would become the first home video game software to sell 1 million units (Sloan, 2011). The console's success would continue, taking the top spot for best-selling toy every year through 1990. NES-related sales were so dominant that in 1989, 16 cents out of every dollar spent on toys went to Nintendo. By 1990, 29 million homes in the United States had Nintendo consoles and five of the top ten selling toys that year were Nintendo products. In part, this was because Nintendo began targeting adults as much as children. At that time, at least 32 percent of the gaming market in the United States was over the age of 18 and at least 25 percent of the market was female (Ramirez, 1990). Though the industry was slow to realize this, Nintendo was not (Nichols, 2014).

But not all was well. Nintendo's success drew complaints and concern, both from parents' groups concerned with video game addiction and competitors focused on unfair competition. It was reported at the time that some retailers were afraid to stock Nintendo competitors, so dominant was Nintendo's position and so aggressive its tactics (Ishizawa, 1992). Central to these was Nintendo's business practices related to software. In order to have a game published on the Nintendo platform, developers had to license with Nintendo who manufactured all its own cartridges. That licensing process gave Nintendo authority to decide when and if a game was published. Each cartridge, in turn, included a microchip for security that allowed the game to play on Nintendo's console (Counsell, 1992). Nintendo argued this was necessary to protect their consoles from the problems that had plagued the industry earlier in the decade, but ironically, this resulted in Atari, which had been hardest hit by shoddy outside development, to sue the company ("Atari Games . . .," 1988). Consumers were also unsatisfied, arguing this drove up the prices of Nintendo games, and a class action lawsuit was filed in California in 1992 (Counsell, 1992). Nintendo would ultimately win these lawsuits ("Nintendo Suit . . .," 1992). There would be a later suit by Nintendo against Atari for patent infringement, similar to a case the company has taken up against toy manufacturer Galoob. Both cases were ultimately resolved, with Nintendo ordered to pay Galoob a settlement for lost profits and with all suits between Nintendo and Atari settled in litigation ("Galoob Wins . . .," 1992; "Nintendo Settles . . .," 1994). Nintendo had also been charged by stated and federal authorities in the United States with price fixing. The company had been accused of forcing retailers to sell their consoles at $99.95 and of delaying shipments to any retailers who sold for less. Ultimately the company agreed to issue $5 coupons for software to consumers who'd registered their console's warranty (Simons, 1991). No doubt this factored into Nintendo's decision to allow some licensees to make their own cartridges (Ramirez, 1990). Game developer and emerging game publisher Electronic Arts (EA) was among the first to receive approval for this.

In addition, the company took on a more active role developing for Europe and Australia, and served as a sales representative for other Nintendo licensees. Prior to that time, Nintendo licensees sold through independent companies; this move was another example of centralization of control on Nintendo's part ("Electronic Arts Announces . . .," 1990).

Competition was heating up as well. In 1990, Nintendo claimed 93 percent of the video game market, while competitors Sega, NEC, and Atari controlled 3.8, 1.3, and 1.2 percent respectively (Ramirez, 1990). The arrival of the 16-bit console generation would change that, and, most surprisingly, Nintendo was not the first out of the gate. Instead, rival company Sega launched its 16-bit console, the Genesis, in August 1989. Nintendo's 16-bit console, the Super Nintendo Entertainment System (SNES), would not arrive for another year. At that time, sales of the NES and the GameBoy had begun to plateau, with the company selling 16.6 million machines in Japan and another 28.8 million in the United States (Ishizawa, 1992). That gave Nintendo sales of $3.96 billion and profits of over $1.1 billion for that same year (Counsell, 1992). But Sega's initial joust was limited to the North American market. By March 1991, Nintendo's market share of hardware would drop to 70 percent in Japan and the United States while its share of software sales dropped to 90 percent (Ishizawa, 1992).

The drop in software sales might not seem significant, but at the time it was estimated that as much as 70 percent of Nintendo's profits came from software sales and licensing royalties. Those royalties alone amounted to between $16 and $24 per cartridge. Sega seemed to have the advantage. By 1992, there were almost 150 games for the Sega Genesis, while the SNES had less than 20. So powerful was Sega that when it decreased prices of the Genesis, Nintendo was forced to follow suit, a first for the company. And when Sega introduced a CD reader for its console, Nintendo was caught flatfooted and was unable to get its version into the market until the following year (Ishizawa, 1992). The move to CDs marked an important shift to the industry, opening new possibilities for game design and eventually the expansion of what consoles were capable of (Nichols, 2014).

In spite of these drops in fortune, Nintendo was still expected to earn more than Hitachi in 1992 (Ishizawa, 1992). In fact, Nintendo was earning pretax earnings of more than $1 billion per year (Sheff, 1993). The company's brand recognition had skyrocketed as well, with Nintendo eclipsing Sony as recognized household product name in the United States (Mizuno, 1993). This allows the company to begin to expand globally, opening three European units focused on retail and distribution in London, Paris, and Utrecht ("Nintendo Starts . . .," 1993). The company's revenue during this period was even more reliant on software, with estimates suggesting that games and software accounted for 99.6 percent of its revenue. Diversification was not a priority for the company, as Yamauchi argued that the diversification so common in other industries – particularly other media industries – was no guarantee of success. But neither did the company assume its reliance on games was foolproof.

Should a million-dollar game not appear, Yamauchi was said to have kept cash reserves on hand sufficient to pay the company's staff for three years. This was possible, however, because the company maintained a very small staff of approximately 900 employees, with most of the company's production – both hardware and software – outsourced (Mizuno, 1993). One crucial adaptation Nintendo explored was outsourcing to China, where the cheaper labor costs could be used to offset the loss of market share ("Nintendo to Make . . .," 1993). At that time, Nintendo's entry into China required partnership with local companies and functioned as a joint venture in the Shenzhen special economic zone, a part of the Guangdong province, and this move marked Nintendo's first attempt at manufacturing overseas. The joint venture was set up with goals to manufacture 10 million consoles a year ("Nintendo to Make . . .," 1993). The Shenzhen zone was the first of the economic development zones set up by China, and it grew to become not only the most successful of the zones but also one of the most successful areas in China, in part owing largely to the number of high-tech companies that based some of their manufacturers there (Kent, n.d.; "Shenzhen's Success . . .," n.d.). In addition to Nintendo, Shenzhen has included development for other important technological companies including Tencent, Huawei, and Foxconn (Kent, n.d.).

Sega's competition forced Nintendo to adapt in another crucial way. Part of the tight control the company had maintained on software production saw developers limited to three game titles the company would allow them to release in a given year. But as console competition heated up and Nintendo lost market share, such limits risked driving developers to their rivals. In response in 1993, Nintendo removed its restriction in hopes of keeping more developers working with them and increasing the chances of finding more of the million-dollar games the company relied so heavily upon. In addition, the company relaxed requirements on how many units of games had to be ordered by developers from 10,000 units to 5,000. But the company only gave up some of its power over developers, who were still on the hook to pay half of Nintendo's commission fee of 20,000 yen per software title manufactured. So effective was this arrangement that it was adopted by other console manufacturers including Sega ("Nintendo Easing . . .," 1994).

The move into China exposed Nintendo to one of the growing problems of the industry: piracy. Estimates suggested that in 1995, China had roughly 20 million illegal SNES consoles, a number that rivaled the installed base of the console in the United States at the same time, while the number of pirated game cartridges was estimated at 100 million or more. Cartridge piracy was estimated to cost publishers as much as $1.5 billion annually, though some estimates put it at closer to $2.5 billion ("100 Million . . .," 1995; "Game Piracy Put . . .," 1996). CDs were not immune either. In 1995, there were just over 250 CD and CD-ROM manufacturing plants in the world, 30 of which were in China, where almost 60 percent of what was manufactured was pirated software ("100 Million . . .," 1995). Nintendo's response was twofold. First, the company urged action through trade groups and international trade piracy to help head off the impact ("Nintendo Urges . . .," 1996). In keeping with this, the company took advantage of the 1946 U.S. Lanham Act, which allowed companies operating in the United States to sue offshore companies suspected of intellectual property (IP) violations in U.S. courts. The company's second strategy involved selling their products at considerable markdown, with software selling for 50 percent or less of what they did in other markets ("100 Million . . .," 1995).

With the combination of increasing competition and the impact of piracy, Nintendo saw its profits begin to decline. In fiscal year 1994, its profits fell 15 percent to 97.8 billion yen, and sales declined by 25 percent from the previous year ("Nintendo Profits Tumble . . .," 1995). And while its pretax profits were down 40 percent from 1991, it still earned more than the much larger Matsushita Electronics, which had 50 times as many employees ("Company Complex . . .," 1996). The SNES had sold 15 million units by March 1995, and sales were dropping (Mitsuada, 1995). By the end of the year, the SNES total units sold exceeded 15 million in Japan and were approaching 40 million globally (Ishibashi, 1996). The company's 32-bit Virtual Boy, released in the middle of 1995, also fell short of expectations, selling only 200,000 units in the first quarter of its release (Mitsuada, 1995). The console would be discontinued the following year, having sold approximately 140,000 units in Japan and 770,000 units worldwide, making it Nintendo's biggest console failure to date (Edwards, 2015). The console which offered 3D graphics, a move toward virtual reality, had been a long, costly project for Nintendo which had purchased the exclusive rights to the technology four years prior. But it also saw the company connecting with video rental stores like Blockbuster Video, in attempt to generate alternative revenue and potentially reaching audiences unable or unwilling to purchase the new console (Flanagan, 2018). By the end of fiscal year 1996, Nintendo's market share was estimated to have dropped to 36 percent globally (Ishibashi, 1996).

Although the failure of the Virtual Boy and the loss of market share were severe, Nintendo was far from out of the game. In fact, from 1982 to at least 1996, Nintendo required no outside funding – loans from banks – owing to decisions about maintaining cash reserves and its tight controls over production and distribution. The company also eschewed traditional Japanese corporate networks – called keiretsu – in which groups of companies were linked together through cross-investment or other interplay of capital ("Company Complex . . .," 1996). While that allowed Nintendo significant independence, it also meant it had smaller margin of error and would have to engineer its own recovery. To do so, the company would need to keep up with the burgeoning console wars.

Nintendo's next console also experienced a series of setbacks, however. The company had been working on its next console, the Nintendo 64 (or N64) since 1993, intending to release the 64-bit console in 1995. But the company had to delay the launch until June 1996 in Japan and September 1996 in the United States (Ishibashi, 1996). The delay was particularly damaging because a new competitor, Sony, had entered the console market in 1994 with its first console, the PlayStation. By the end of 1996, Sony had double Nintendo's installed base for that console generation, with more than 11 million units shipped, outpacing Sega's 7 million and Nintendo's roughly 4 million (Ishibashi, 1997). With such competition, even Nintendo's advantage in Japan had dropped considerably. In 1992, the company had approximately 90 percent of the Japanese market, but by 1996, it had dropped to roughly 40 percent (Ishibashi, 1996). Perhaps the most striking marker of this shift was the number of software developers who switched allegiance, no longer developing exclusively for Nintendo. These included Enix, Square, Konami, Taito, Capcom, Midway, Acclaim, and Electronic Arts (Ryan, 2011; Yamazaki, 1997).

Much of the delay owed to Nintendo's goal of expanding the capabilities of their consoles. While previous consoles had already incorporated modems, the N64 was the company's first attempt at adding an external drive to double memory. In addition, the company was working with a new Silicon graphics chip set which was designed to be of low cost and to also allow for 3D graphics (Ryan, 2011). But the delay had been felt in other ways. By 1997, only 15 software titles were available for the N64 in Japan. Less were available in the United States, though sales of the console were almost double (Yamazaki, 1997). In contrast, Sony had 500 titles available for the PlayStation ("Nintendo Takes Off . . .," 1997).

Once these delays were overcome, however, the N64 helped Nintendo regain some its dominance. By the end of 1996, Nintendo had shipped less than 2 million units of the N64. But in the first half of 1997 alone, the company shipped more than 6 million units. By the end of the year, Nintendo planned to ship 1 million units monthly. This wasn't enough to catch Sony, which had shipped 10 million PlayStations in Japan alone by the end of 1997; it reestablished Nintendo as a major force in the market ("Nintendo Takes Off . . .," 1997). Even with the slow rollout and the limited number of games available, the company's net profits rose more than 9 percent in fiscal year 1996 (Yamazaki, 1997). This was particularly impressive as the company dropped the prices of the N64 by a third to help draw audiences away from the PlayStation ("Nintendo Takes Off . . .," 1997).

The console proved particularly popular in the United States, and its popularity over the Sega Saturn was instrumental in rival Sega's decline and eventual exit from the console market after the release of its next console, the Sega Dreamcast (Olenick, 1999; Nichols, 2014). Though the Dreamcast sold well, the release of Sony's PlayStation 2 and Nintendo's GameCube, combined with the challenge posed when Microsoft released its first console, would push the company out of the console market (Inside the Internet, 2000). Microsoft's first console, the Xbox was released in November 2001, just days before Nintendo would release its GameCube ("Game Industry Pins . . .," 2001). By 1999, the

PlayStation was the dominant console globally, having sold more than 50 million units compared to the N64's 20 million (Naito, 1999). The company's bigger success was the continued popularity of its handheld GameBoy, which continued to be a leader in sales of hardware and software despite having been in the market for roughly 10 years ("Game Industry Pins . . .," 2001). Estimates suggested that in that decade, the GameBoy had sold more than 110 million units worldwide (Sloan, 2011).

But all was not well within Nintendo. It was reported that there was conflict over how Yamauchi's son-in-law, Minoru Arakawa, who headed Nintendo of America had been running the subsidiary, particularly the practice of obtaining sizable loans which cut against Yamauchi's desire to avoid debt and maintain cash on hand (Unozawa, 2002). The Kyoto branch of Nintendo, overseen by Yamauchi, had been responsible for overseeing console and software development, while marketing and sales tended to be driven by Nintendo of America (Sloan, 2011). Arakawa had seemed the natural successor to Yamauchi, who had been working toward retirement, but had lost favor with his father-in-law for his spending and a perceived lack of drive (Ryan, 2011). The choices were limited, as Yamauchi had maintained extremely tight levels of control. He was solely responsible for setting sales volumes and prices across the range of Nintendo's geographic markets, and the board which advised him was small, almost all of whom were internal to the company. At the age of 74, Yamauchi stepped down in May 2002, also changing the structure of the company's board ("Long-time Nintendo . . .," 2002). The same year he retired, the number of members increased from four to six, adding Shigeru Miyamoto, the famed developer of so many of Nintendo's hit games, and Genyo Takeda. Satoru Iwata, who had headed software development company HAL Laboratory, a longtime Nintendo ally, became Nintendo's new president at the age of 42 (Unozawa, 2002; DeWinter, 2015; "Long-time Nintendo . . .," 2002). Iwata had been hired by Nintendo in 2000 as the head of its management and planning sections ("Long-time Nintendo . . .," 2002). At that time, Nintendo's estimated worth was more than $20 billion (Sloan, 2011).

Iwata took control of the company at a critical moment. The GameCube had recently launched, and despite the 2001 launch of the GameBoy Advance, the company was already working on the handheld's successor, the Nintendo DS ("Nintendo Readies Advanced . . .," 2000). The GameBoy Advance could be used in conjunction with the new GameCube console, a feature that would be used in later combinations by Nintendo to much success (Koyama, 2001). The 32-bit device advanced saw a staggered release, launching in March 2001 in Japan, and in July 2001 in the North American and European markets ("Nintendo Readies Advanced . . .," 2000). The DS came from the handheld's dual screens, were seen as vital to the company's success (Sloan, 2011). The GameCube launched first in Japan, on September 14, 2001, and just a few weeks later, November 18, 2001, in North America. The company intended to ship 4 million units of the console by March 2002, and priced the console at 25,000 yen in Japan and $199.95 in the United States (Koyama, 2001). The company hoped worldwide sales of the GameCube would reach 50 million by March 2005 (Unozawa, 2002).

But fiscal year 2002 showed the company a different reality, with its operating profits dropping roughly 16 percent to 1001.1 billion yen, as its sales dropped by 9 percent to 504.1 billion yen. Still the company had considerable cash on hand – approximately 750 billion yen – to help them survive the downturn. In this period, sales of games including games for their handhelds, accounted for just over 50 percent of the company's earnings. These drops prompted the company to consider ways to expand their markets. Such a move was crucial, as most analysts agreed the video game industry had matured, making adaptation a necessity. Again, China was seen as a strong potential avenue to pursue, though the risks were great ("Nintendo Flush . . .," 2003). By 2003, the company had again entered the Chinese market, selling consoles and software. But the company was wary because of the impact Chinese piracy had already had on its bottom line (Nakanishi, 2003a). In 2002, it was estimated that the company lost almost 78.7 billion yen in sales due to software piracy in China ("Nintendo Flush . . .," 2003). This made the move strategic, with Nintendo recognizing the growing importance the Chinese market would play and, so, the company sought to tie up distribution channels before its competitors (Nakanishi, 2003a).

Beyond its expansion into China, the company worked to create alliances within the industry. Owing to the changing reality of the industry and the strength of its competitors, 2003 saw Nintendo take the extraordinary move of creating cooperative agreements with Namco, Sega, Bandai, and a range of other game companies, many of which had been staunch rivals previously ("Nintendo Creates New . . .," 2004). The company also began to invest in microchip manufacture, something many console manufacturers began to seriously invest in.

Nintendo invested $15 million in a U.S. startup in 2003, working to develop large-capacity memory chips for its machines ("Nintendo Flush . . .," 2003). Perhaps most crucially, the company changed its marketing strategy, focusing primarily on children and families as their core demographic and beginning to take advantage of trend surveys to help shape its approach. However, the company resisted moving into online gaming despite what seemed clear affinities, indicating they felt the market wasn't yet profitable. In spite of these moves, the company continued to see its dominance erode, taking its first net loss since 1962 in fiscal year 2003. That loss totaled 2.8 billion yen ("Nintendo Creates . . .," 2004).

While the GameBoy maintained its success, having sold 33 million units by the middle of 2003, the GameCube was less successful. Recognizing the importance of continued innovation, Nintendo was already working on the successor to the GameCube by 2003, though it also worked to leverage the success of the GameBoy to help the GameCube. To do so, the company began seeking game development for software that could be played on both machines. Unfortunately this didn't prove to be enough, and ultimately, the GameCube was seen as a failure for the company in part because it didn't adopt some of the newly available features other consoles were using, such as the ability to play media other than games (Nakanishi, 2003b). The failure pushed the company to consider what it might do to both boost sales and expand its customer base ("Nintendo Creates . . ., 2004). The company's next handheld console, the Nintendo DS, was just such an attempt ("Interview: Originality . . .," 2004). In addition, under Iwata's direction, the company began to survey customers over the Internet to better gauge their interest in products. The struggles of the GameCube led to the company's taking a substantial net loss of approximately 2.8 billion yen during the first quarter of fiscal year 2003, the company's first such loss since it went public ("Nintendo Creates . . .," 2004).

As had been the pattern, the arrival of a new piece of hardware marked Nintendo's attempt to rebound from this loss. At the end of 2004, the company released its new handheld, the Nintendo DS ("Portable Game . . .," 2004). But the release faced a new challenge: the company's rival Sony released its first attempt at a portable console at the same time: the PlayStation Portable or the PSP (Portable Game . . .," 2004). The PSP was released in mid-December while the DS was released in November in the North American market, and in early December in Japan. In December 2004 alone, the console sold 1.4 million units, pushing the company to increase the number of Chinese contractors it worked with in order to make more units available during the holiday buying season ("Portable Game . . .," 2004). The DS was priced at 15,000 yen when it was released ("Game Industry Prays . . .," 2004).

The handheld market was booming. In 2002, handhelds accounted for only 20 percent of the Japanese market, and a similar percentage globally, and by 2005, they made up 47 percent ("Portable Game . . .," 2006). Sales of the DS stayed high, eclipsing those of the PSP. By 2006, DS yearly sales had doubled, with almost 11.5 million units being shipped globally ("Nintendo Profit . . .," 2006). In the Japanese market, portable sales marked another milestone, eclipsing the sales of consoles for the first time during the January to June half of fiscal year 2006 ("Portable Game . . .," 2006). This was a boon for Nintendo, which reported another boom cycle with pretax profits for the year growing by 11 percent to 160.7 billion yen for 2006. In that period, sales of all portable consoles – which included both the DS and the still supported Game-Boy Advance – rose to 223.8 billion yen, a growth of more than 8 percent, while software sales grew by 19 percent to 172.6 billion ("Nintendo Profit . . .," 2006). As a way to keep the DS line fresh, the company released a new version, the DS Lite, in March 2006, but sales of the original continued to be high ("Fans Rush . . .," 2006). Nintendo President Iwata noted in an interview that the company was still shipping 150,000 units of the DS and that they continued to sell quickly ("Interview: Forsaking . . .," 2006).

The company's strategy to expand its audience base paid dividends with the DS line. The company's surveys showed that returning players accounted for more than 40 percent of buyers of the DS, leading the company to lean into their nostalgia redeploying and adapting games from their previous systems for use on the DS (Kawai, 2007; Fukuyama, 2006). Previous console and handheld titles as well as arcade games from a number of the company's allies including Namco Bandai and Square Enix were developed to play on the DS. *New Super Mario Bros.* was one such game, released in 2006, and was one of the most successful launches. Based on the original *Mario Bros.* released in 1983 for the Famicom/NES, which sold more than 40 million units over the product's lifetime, the new game was shipped more than 1 million units in its first week (Fukuyama, 2006). *New Super Marios Bros.* sold more than 4 million units by May 2007, while Square Enix's remake of *Final Fantasy III* for the DS sold more than 1 million units between its release and May 2007. The process of converting old games to new consoles is one that a number of developers noted was considerably cheaper, costing tens of millions of yen instead of hundreds (Kawai, 2007). Indeed, the DS was a prime example of an approach to consoles championed under Yamauchi and continued under Iwata: the idea that bigger and more capable was automatically better ("Interview: Originality . . .," 2004). This was clearly part of the approach to the next console Nintendo would release as well.

In November 2006, the company released its new console, the Wii. Selling for 25,000 yen in Japan and $250 in the United States, the Wii began with a slate of 60 titles, and Nintendo intended to add to the software library for the console with 10 titles per month after launch ("Nintendo Gives Details . . .," 2006). To help it compete with Sony's PlayStation 3, the company shipped 400,000 units at launch, more than quadruple of Sony's offering ("Nintendo Set to . . .," 2006). Iwata noted that part of the challenge the company took on in developing the Wii was to create a console that anyone in the family from age 5 to 95 could play, particularly one that would appeal to mothers ("Interview: Forsaking . . .," 2006; "Console Makers . . .," 2007). Centering its strategy around creating a console that would appeal to "females . . ., friends . . ., and foreign markets" the Wii marked a distinct difference from other consoles being manufactured at the time ("Console Makers . . .," 2007). The Wii's functionality was distinct, using motion tracking technology in its controllers allowed developers to approach games in a different way, and this approach marked a crucial distinction in the company's approach in coming years (Jones and Thiruvathukal, 2019). Nintendo's approach to the Wii involved a mix of off-the-shelf technologies, years of research, rethinking console audiences, and developments in motion tracking to create a very different user experience ("Interview: Forsaking . . .," 2006). In fact, many a time when other console manufacturers were developing their own proprietary microchips, Nintendo was using commonly available microchips which only cost a few hundred yen each for many of the functions in the Wii (Nichols, 2014; Saijo, 2007). Nintendo's continued use of relatively cheap, off-the-shelf technologies was particularly important for the Wii, as the company continued its strategy of relying on a number of outside suppliers for both the parts needed as well as outsourcing the manufacture itself. For example, the key component in the Wii controller was a triaxial accelerator sensor which was a relatively inexpensive technology purchased from a number of U.S. companies including Analogue Devices, Inc ("Nintendo Uses . . .," 2008). Indeed, at the time, the company owned no factories of its own, but outsourced everything about the manufacturing of its consoles (Saijo, 2007). In contrast, production of the company's consoles was handled by Hon Hai Precision Industry Co. of Taiwan and a few other reliable firms ("Nintendo Uses . . .," 2008). The reliance on outside manufacturing and outsourcing freed up Nintendo's own engineers to focus on game development itself ("Nintendo Uses . . .," 2008).

Sales of the Wii were particularly impressive in 2007, spiking to 18.61 million units, a 220 percent increase from the previous year, while software jumped by 310 percent, to a total of 119.6 million units ("Nintendo Continues . . .," 2008). At the same time, sales of the DS were beginning to fall in Japan, dropping to 6.94 million units ("Nintendo Enjoys . . .," 2008). That led to a 120 percent increase in profits for the company, earning them 487.2 billion yen ("Nintendo Continues . . .," 2008). The console continued to be a huge success for Nintendo, selling more than 20 million units worldwide in its first two years ("Nintendo Uses . . .," 2008). This resulted in the company adjusting its projections, hoping to sell 14 million units in fiscal year 2008, a jump of 140 percent ("Console Makers Setting . . .," 2007). The demand for the Wii was so high in Nintendo's key markets – Japan, North American, and Europe – that the company delayed releasing the console in other Asian markets until 2008 in spite of manufacturing more than 1.8 million units a month. This meant the South Korean and Chinese markets, despite their size and fervor, were left years behind in the company's plans. South Korea experienced less of a lag in console releases, with the DS having been available; in contrast, the company was offering the N64 and older consoles in China via a joint venture ("In Brief: Nintendo . . .," 2007). The success of the DS and Wii vaulted Nintendo back into the stratosphere, with Nintendo's market-capitalization surpassing Canon, Inc.'s to become the second only to Toyota Motor Corp. among Japanese companies at that time (Saijo, 2007).

In the North American and European markets, DS sales continued to grow (Watanabe, 2008b). By 2008, nearly 90 percent of Nintendo sales came from outside Japan. Roughly half of Nintendo's sales were coming from the North American market, but Europe was increasingly important, topping sales from both North and South America for the first time in 2008. European sales earned Nintendo almost 362 billion yen, just in the April to September period, while sales from the Americas came to 330.6 billion yen in the same period (Watanabe, 2008a). Analysts pointed to the demand for Nintendo products as the key driver of both the European and American markets through 2008 (Kanematsu, 2009). Nintendo had sold more than 77 million DS units worldwide by 2008, though the handheld was still selling out in many parts of the world. At the time, it was assumed that the typical lifespan of a handheld was three to four years, but as the DS approached its fifth-year, sales were so strong globally that Nintendo often repeated a mantra of wanting to achieve "one machine per person." Given that the typically DS owning household boasted 2.8 users and 1.8 machines, there was good reason for believing Nintendo could sell more of the profitable handheld even as it was working on the DS successor (Watanabe, 2008b).

That successor, the DSi, arrived in October 2008. The DSi was a souped version of the DS, with the addition of a camera and music player built in (Watanabe, 2008b). No doubt this partly owed to the ascendancy of the Apple iPod and iPhone. Indeed, combined sales of the DS and DS Lite had topped 31 million units by 2008, well past the 20 million mark that had widely been assumed to be the saturation point for handheld game machines ("Nintendo Continues . . .," 2008; Watanabe and Hirooka, 2008). Software for the DS, too, had boomed: there were more than 900 software titles available for the handheld (Hasegawa, 2008). Building on that success, the company began to envision other uses for the console, as Iwata put it, the console needs to be approached as "capable of enriching people's lives, rather than merely a games console." Such alternative uses included being used as an information terminal at museums and other public spaces such as the Nintendo SafeCo Field, as an educational tool, for use in rehabilitation by hospitals, and as a distribution device for partner Dai Nippon Printing Co.'s anime and comics (Watanabe, 2008c).

With both its handheld and its console selling well, Nintendo sales skyrock-eted. During fiscal year 2007, the company's sales reached a record 1.63 trillion yen, more than two times the sales from 2005 ("Nintendo Uses . . .," 2008). Most of this growth was attributed to the DS, as the Wii was still relatively new to the market, though fiscal year 2007 was the first time the Wii contributed to earnings for entire fiscal year ("Nintendo Expects . . .," 2007; "Nintendo Continues . . .," 2008). Taking advantage of its position, the company also looked at acquiring a number of companies, settling on Monolith Software, which had been owned by Namco Bandai Holdings, Inc. Iwata noted that while the company was often seen as hesitant to acquire companies, that the company was always looking to acquire but would only do so "in cases where doing so will help in securing parts essential for future growth, including adding special functions to [their] hardware" ("Nintendo's Iwata . . .," 2007). As a company, Apple had emerged not only as a competitor but also as a touch stone for comparison. It was noted in the press, for example, that the companies shared similar approaches to manu-facture and, more impressively, that Nintendo's profit to sales ratio in 2008 was 23 percent higher than that of Apple. Similarly, Nintendo's small size – still just over 3,000 employees in 2008 – gave the company an operating profit per employee of more than 130 million yen, which was four times larger than com-petitor Microsoft, making the company a world leader in that regard ("Nintendo

Uses . . .," 2008). In that same year, the company was estimated to have cash reserves in excess of 1 trillion yen ("Nintendo Continues . . ., 2008).

Such reserves remained necessary, as the company saw sales of the Wii drop sharply off after 2008. From its release to 2008, the console had sold 40 million units globally (Wii Deliver, 2009). In the North and South American markets, sales dropped by 38 percent, while European sales dropped nearly 50 percent. Overall, sales of the console fell off by roughly 57 percent globally. With the slide in console sales came a hit to their profit, which dropped by 66 percent from 2007 to 2008 ("Nintendo Embarks . . .," 2009). Even so, Nintendo's market share in several foreign markets grew. In the United States, Nintendo controlled 47 percent of the market while in the United Kingdom, France, and Germany, they controlled 55 percent. And foreign sales still dominated for the company, growing from 7 percent in the same period to account 87.5 percent of the company's total (Tsutsumi, 2009). In part, this owed to increased attention to some of those markets. Starting in fiscal year 2007, the company began spending larger amounts on advertising in a number of territories. In Europe in particular, the company increased its ad spending by 40 percent in fiscal year 2007 alone (Watanabe, 2008a).

In keeping with previous consoles, Nintendo worked to maximize the value of the Wii, entering arrangements with a number of companies to expand how the console might be used. Among these were Nippon Telephone and Telegraph East Co. and Nippon Telephone and Telegraph West Co. to bring news and information over data lines with the two companies. The company also worked with Dentsu Inc. to bring family-oriented entertainment content via the Wii, hoping to make it a central piece of the living room (Wii Deliver, 2009). At the same time, the company needed to find a way to increase sales. For the Wii, this meant a price cut: in October 2009 the company introduced 20 percent on the Wii (Hanai, 2009). But it also meant the company needed to consider introducing a new piece of hardware: the handheld 3DS. Introduced six years after the original DS, the 3DS not only built on the previous console's success but also drew on years of research. The handheld was a costly one, however; priced at 25,000 yen in Japan, it was 25 percent more expensive than the Wii (Oikawa, 2010). At the introduction of the 3DS, the company knew the handheld would not be a major contributor to the company until 2011 or later ("Nintendo Looks . . .," 2010). That would prove to be a long wait and the start of a particularly rough period for the company, in spite of numbers that showed amazing growth. In 2008, the company's sales were 28 times larger than that in 1983, and its operating profit was 27 times larger (Kanematsu, 2010).

Even as the company's share of the vital North American market rose, with the company accounting for 53.5 percent of the games market and 60.8 percent of the console market there, its earnings began to drop off sharply (Kanematsu, 2010). The company's operating profits fell off by 36 percent to 356.5 billion yen, while sales dropped 22 percent to 1.43 trillion yen ("Nintendo Looks . . .,"

2010). This posed a significant and relatively unheard of problem for the company. Between the release of its first console in 1983 and 2008, the company only experienced declines in both sales and profits for multiple years twice: from 1994 to 1995 and from 2000 to 2001. At both points it was the release of a new Sony console that was the major factor (Kanematsu, 2010). This time, however, it was overseas rival Apple and the rise of smartphones that was the culprit. This led to shareholders beginning to push the company to find a way to enter the mobile games market, something Nintendo has been seen as hesitant to do historically (Carew, 2016). Given the company's reliance on casual gamers, finding a strategy that accounted for the rise of smartphone games was needed. Analysts noted that a reliance on casual gamers risks the audience shrinking, as casual gamers have been seen as prone to quitting gaming once they lose interest in the games that drew them to a platform initially. The boom in free titles for smartphones and online games only exacerbated these risks. Those factors combined, resulting in fewer hit titles being released for Nintendo's platforms, it spelled trouble (Kanematsu, 2010).

In fiscal 2010, group net profit continued to fall, dropping by 66 percent to 76.6 billion yen. Sales, too, continued to fall, dropping to 1.01 trillion yen, roughly $12.3 billion (Oikawa, 2011b). By March 2011, there had been roughly 86 million Wiis sold worldwide, an amazing number, but one that also suggested market saturation. In part, owing to high levels of piracy in emerging markets like China and much of Asia, approximately 85 percent of the company's sales were coming from developed nations, and its profile in countries like China and India remained quite small. Rival company Sony dealt with this by selling one generation behind in developing countries: while the PlayStation 3 was sold in the major markets the PlayStation 2 was sold in developing countries. Nearly half of the Wiis sold were accounted for by North America alone (Sese and Oikawa, 2011). As its consoles aged, software continued to be the primary contributors to the company's success. Analysts noted this was likely the case for all console makers in light of the growing popularity of the iPhone and other smartphones (Oikawa, 2011a). As evidence of the outsize importance of software, the company pointed to the introduction of a dance game as the primary reason for a slight increase in Wii sales in the United States in this period (Sese and Oikawa, 2011).

In the summer of 2011, Nintendo truly hit hard times. After topping the Nikkei bonus ranking for the third straight year, paying an average of 1.62 million yen to each employee, the company had to cut back (Oikawa, 2011c). By the end of fiscal year 2011, sales were down almost 40 percent from the previous year, while sales fell almost 10 percent ("Nintendo Agonizes . . .," 2012). In response, the management began to seek cuts throughout the company, including encouraging workers to be mindful of the cost of utilities and canceling a number of employee perks (Hayakawa, 2012). Midway through the year, the company reported another loss of 17.2 billion yen, which was a slight improvement on the previous year. The 3DS handheld, which the company had hoped to begin having a significant impact on profits, had sold 19.2 million units and sales seemed appeared to be on the rise ("Nintendo Agonizes . . .," 2012). The company also had high hopes for the Nintendo Wii U, which was released at the end of 2012. The console had two versions: an 8 GB and a 32 GB version. The former was sold for 26,500 yen in Japan and $299.99 in the United States, while the latter was sold for 31,500 yen and $349.99 (Watanabe, 2012). As with previous consoles, the company was prepared to lose money on initial sales of the Wii U, and estimates suggested that the company lost roughly 10,000 yen on each unit sold in the early going (Hayakawa, 2012). In part, this strategy was geared toward trying to continue to broaden its audience ("Nintendo Agonizes . . .," 2012). Part of what the company struggled with owed to the response it and many Japanese game makers had to developing games. With each console generation, the cost of developing games went up. Estimates at the time suggested that Microsoft had spent in excess of 10 billion yen or $128 billion on the *Halo* franchise; in contrast, Japanese game makers were estimated to spend an average of 100 million yen on developing new games (Hayashi, 2012). As Nintendo president Satoru Iwata noted, it was Nintendo's practice to "handle both hardware and software" and to use both to generate profits ("Interview: Unique . . .," 2012). A problem in one resulted in challenges for the other, and if both struggled, so, too, would Nintendo (Watanabe, 2012).

Unfortunately, that was exactly what happened. As Iwata was quoted on the eve of the 30th anniversary of the Famicom, the challenge of convincing users to pay the usual prices for video game software was only getting harder in the face of increased pressure from smartphones ("Nintendo Crisis . . .," 2013). Barely a year since the release of the Wii U, the company was already forced to drop its price, and it released more basic versions of both the Wii and the 3DS, called the Wii mini and the 2DS, respectively, in an attempt to bolster sales ("Nintendo to Offer . . .," 2013; "Nintendo's Downsized . . .," 2013). It was the company's hope that sales from software for the Wii mini, in particular, might offset some of its losses, as it would be able to take advantage of the more than 1,200 titles available for the Wii platform ("Nintendo's Downsized . . .," 2013). Moreover, the company understood the first management reshuffle in 11 years, notably decreasing the average age of its board members by almost seven years ("Ninendo Crisis . . .," 2013). Management took another hit in September 2013, when former president Hiroshi Yamauchi passed away. Though he had resigned as president, he had continued to serve as advisor to his hand-picked replacement, Satoru Iwata ("Slow to Adapt . . .," 2014). The company had yet to settle on a plan for their smartphone problem, though investors continued to urge the company to enter that arena. In part, there was concern about the cost of redesigning Nintendo's classic games for smartphones because many of them were designed for Nintendo's increasingly unique controls. Moreover, analysts noted that while the company's IP, particularly best-selling and long-running franchises, would make a mint on smartphones, the company would likely struggle in the short term as it adjusted to both different models of pricing and much lower fees (Hayashi and Fujiwara, 2014).

Nintendo continued to work, with Iwata announcing the company was developing its next console, codenamed the NX, with an eye to releasing it in 2016 ("Nintendo Loses . . .," 2015). With the Wii U selling a meager 13.5 million units by 2017, the company would need another hit (Suruga, 2017). The NX would be that hit, albeit under a different name: the Nintendo Switch. Following the upheavals at the company, the Switch would be released in early 2017. Sadly, before it could be released Iwata passed away from a bile duct tumor in July 2015, forcing another adjustment to the company's leadership ("Nintendo Loses . . .," 2015).

Conclusion

From its origins as a manufacturer of hanufada playing cards to a globally dominant fixture in the video game industry, Nintendo has been remarkably consistent in its approach. Of particular emphasis has been the company's acknowledgment that the business of video games is not one which produces necessities. From its beginning as a family-owned company, Nintendo remained lean, focusing on affordable production and innovation with its products, while working to ensure that it would be able to survive downturns in the market. These guiding principles allowed the company to weather a world war, leadership upheaval, and changes to the games industry itself. Sometimes this meant choices that ran counter to prevailing trends within the industry. Along the way, the company recognized the value of IP, first through its licensing from other companies and, ultimately, developing its own. As will be seen in subsequent chapters, these themes resonate with both Nintendo's business practices and how it has sought to maintain both its cultural and its political influence. Chapter 3 elaborates on how these specific approaches have been turned into practices by the company, allowing it to develop a portfolio of extremely well-recognized and profitable IP. Chapter 4 examines how the company has wielded its power to protect and grow that IP, helping to shape the video game industry as it continues to grow.

Note

1 Also sometimes spelled Chitory.

References

100 Million (Pirated) Nintendo Games in China. (1995). *Consumer Electronics*, 1.
American Firm Obtains Sales Rights of Donkey Kong Video Games. (1982). *Jiji Press Ticker Service*. NexisUni.

And the Winner Are . . .. (1983). *United Press International*. NexisUni.

Ashcraft, B. (2011). The Nintendo They've Tried to Forget: Gambling, Gangsters, and Love Hotels. *Kotaku*. Retrieved June 9, 2021, from https://kotaku.com/the-nintendo-theyve-tried-to-forget-gambling-gangster-5784314

Atari Games Launches Double-Barreled Attack on Nintendo. (1988). *The Associated Press*. NexisUni.

Atari Inc. (1984). Planning to Pull Out of the Japanese Market. *The Japan Economic Journal*. NexisUni.

Atari Signs License Contract with Nintendo. (1983). *Jiji Press Ticker Service*. NexisUni.

Carew, R. (2016, July 13). Fund's Nintendo Bet Pays Off. *Wall Street Journal Asia*. ProQuest Newsstand.

Cohen, S. (1984). *Zap! The Rise and Fall of Atari*. New York: McGraw-Hill.

Coleco's New Video Challenge. (1982). *The New York Times*. NexisUni.

Company Complex as Its Games. (1996). *The Nikkei Weekly (Japan)*. NexisUni.

Console Makers Setting New Parameters for Game Market. (2007). *The Nikkei Weekly (Japan)*. NexisUni.

Counsell, G. (1992). The Only Game in Town. *The Independent (London)*. NexisUni.

Demaria, R. (2003). *High Score: The Illustrated History of Electronic Games* (2nd ed.). New York: McGraw Hill Osbourne Media.

DeWinter, J. (2015). *Shigeru Miyamoto: Super Mario Bros., Donkey Kong, the Legend of Zelda*. New York: Bloomsbury Academic.

Edwards, B. (2015, August 21). *Unraveling The Enigma of Nintendo's Virtual Boy, 20 Years Later*. Fast Company. https://www.fastcompany.com/3050016/unraveling-the-enigma-of-nintendos-virtual-boy-20-years-later

Electronic Arts Announces Expansion Strategy into Nintendo Video Game Market: Company Places First Order, Starts Development on GameBoy. (1990). *PR Newswire*. NexisUni.

Fans Rush to Buy Nintendo DS Lite. (2006). *The Nikkei Weekly (Japan)*. NexisUni.

Flanagan, G. (2018, March 6). *The Incredible Story of the "Virtual Boy" – Nintendo's VR Headset from 1995 that Failed Spectacularly*. Business Insider. https://www.businessinsider.com/nintendo-virtual-boy-reality-3d-video-games-super-mario-2018-3

Fukuyama, E. (2006). Classic Video Games Stage Revival on Nintendo DS. *The Nikkei Weekly (Japan)*. NexisUni.

Galoob Wins $15 Million from Nintendo of America. (1992). *PR Newswire*. NexisUni.

Game Industry Pins Hopes for Revival on New Consoles. (2001). *The Nikkei Weekly (Japan)*. NexisUni.

Game Industry Prays for Hot Winter. (2004). *The Nikkei Weekly (Japan)*. NexisUni.

Game Piracy Put at $2.5 Billion. (1996). *Phillips Business Information's Interactive Video News* (p. 1).

Hanai, Y. (2009). Console Makers Look for Buyers. *The Nikkei Weekly (Japan)*. NexisUni.

Harmetz, A. (1983). Makers Vie for Millions in Home Video Games. *The New York Times*. NexisUni.

Harmetz, A. (1984). Video Arcades' New Hope. *The New York Times*. NexisUni.

Harris, B. J. (2014). *Console Wars: Sega, Nintendo, and the Battle that Defined a Generation* (1st ed.). New York, NY: It Books, An Imprint of HarperCollins Publishers.

Hasegawa, M. (2008). Game Consoles Get Some Class. *The Nikkei Weekly (Japan)*. NexisUni.

Hayakawa, A. (2012). Nintendo Banks on Wii U to Bring Back Good Times. *The Nikkei Weekly (Japan)*. NexisUni.

Hayashi, E. (2012). Japanese Video Game Makers Losing Out as Global Competition Intensifies. *The Nikkei Weekly (Japan)*. NexisUni.

Hayashi, H., & Fujiwara, T. (2014). Nintendo Still Unable to Solve Smartphone Puzzle. *Nikkei Asian Review (Japan)*. NexisUni.

Helwing, D. (1983). Tactics Questioned as Video Game Border War Heats Up. *The Globe and Mail (Canada)*. NexisUni.

IN BRIEF: Nintendo to Start Selling Wii in Asia. (2007). *The Nikkei Weekly (Japan)*. NexisUni.

Inside the Internet. (2000). Sega or Sony: Which Machine Will You Buy? *Inside the Internet, 7*(1), 15.

International Arcade Museum. (2023). *Videogame – Letter: A – A List of All the Machines Ever Made!* https://www.arcade-museum.com/game_list.php?letter=A&type=Videogame

Interview: Forsaking Performance Race, Nintendo Targets Non-Gamers. (2006). *The Nikkei Weekly (Japan)*. NexisUni.

Interview: Originality More Important than Technology. (2004). *The Nikkei Weekly (Japan)*.

Interview: Unique Fun, New Ways to Play Seen as Trick for Wii U's Long-Term Success. (2012). *The Nikkei Weekly (Japan)*. NexisUni.

Ishibashi, A. (1996). Nimble Rivals Bruise Mighty Nintendo Delay of Advanced Machines Shakes Faith of Investors, Customers. *The Nikkei Weekly (Japan)*. NexisUni.

Ishibashi, A. (1997). Game Business Plays Rough Sega-Bandai Merger is Bringing Together Firms Wounded in Fray. *The Nikkei Weekly (Japan)*. NexisUni.

Ishizawa, M. (1992). Nintendo's New Game: Competition; Newcomer Sega's CD-ROM, 16-Bit System Make TV Computer Market a 2-Player Contest. *The Nikkei Weekly (Japan)*. NexisUni.

Iwata Asks: Game & Watch. (2010). *Nintendo of Europe GmbH*. Retrieved June 10, 2021, from https://www.nintendo.co.uk/Iwata-Asks/Iwata-Asks-Game-Watch/Iwata-Asks-Game-Watch/1-When-Developers-Did-Everything/1-When-Developers-Did-Everything-222941.html

Japanese TV Game Makers Take Up Production in U.S. (1982). *The Japan Economic Journal*. NexisUni.

Jones, S. E., & Thiruvathukal, G. K. (2019). *Codename Revolution – The Nintendo Wii Platform*. The MIT Press.

Jurkovich, T. (2020, July 9). Every Nintendo Console Ranked by How Long They Were Supported. *TheGamer*. https://www.thegamer.com/nintendo-consoles-ranked-by-how-long-supported/

Kanematsu, Y. (2009). Market Shrugs at Nintendo's Gains. *The Nikkei Weekly (Japan)*. NexisUni.

Kanematsu, Y. (2010). Mario Not Super Enough as Nintendo Cools Down. *The Nikkei Weekly (Japan)*. NexisUni.

Kawai, T. (2007, May 14). Nostalgia Hooks Veteran Gamers. *The Nikkei Weekly (Japan)*.

Kent, S. L. (2001). *The Ultimate History of Video Games: From Pong to Pokémon and Beyond – The Story Behind the Craze That Touched Our Lives and Changed the World*. Roseville, CA: Prima Publishing.

Kocurek, C. A. (2015). *Coin-Operated Americans*. Minnesota: University of Minnesota Press.

Koyama, T. (2001). Nintendo Goes Back to Basics in New Console. *The Nikkei Weekly (Japan)*. NexisUni.

Long-Time Nintendo President to Step Down at End of Month. (2002). *The Nikkei Weekly (Japan)*. NexisUni.

Matsushita Electric Tops 807 Firms in Consolidated Earnings Figures. (1983). *The Japan Economic Journal*. NexisUni.

Mayra, F. (2008). *An Introduction to Game Studies*. London: SAGE Publications.

McKevitt, A. (2017). *Consuming Japan: Popular Culture and the Globalizing of 1980s America (Studies in United States Culture)*. Chapel Hill: The University of North Carolina Press.

Mitsuada, H. (1995). Kingpin Nintendo Takes Time Out Video-Game Giant's Lack of a Hit 32-Bit Machine Costs It Market Share as Sega, Sony Gain Ground. *The Nikkei Weekly (Japan)*. NexisUni.

Mizuno, Y. (1993). Nintendo Sticks to Its Low-Cost Guns; Despite Analysts' Misgivings, President Pursues Simple Strategy. *The Nikkei Weekly (Japan)*. NexisUni.

Mochizuki, T., & Savov, V. (2020, August 19). Epic's Battle with Apple and Google Actually Dates Back to *Pac-Man. Bloomberg.com*. https://www.bloomberg.com/news/articles/2020-08-19/epic-games-fortnite-battle-with-apple-and-google-can-be-traced-to-nintendo-tax

Naito, M. (1999). Borders Explode in Game Industry as Makers Morph into Global Groups Nintendo, Sega Form Strategic Alliances Outside Sector. *The Nikkei Weekly (Japan)*. NexisUni.

Nakanishi, T. (2003a). Nintendo Takes Game War to China. *The Nikkei Weekly (Japan)*. NexisUni.

Nakanishi, T. (2003b). Nintendo Trails Pack in Game Market. *The Nikkei Weekly (Japan)*.

Nichols, R. (2014). *The Video Game Business (International Screen Industries)*. New York, NY: Palgrave Macmillan on Behalf of the British Film Institute.

Nintendo. (2023). *Nintendo Support: Wii U & Nintendo 3DS eShop Discontinuation Q&A*. https://en-americas-support.nintendo.com/app/answers/detail/a_id/57847/~/wii-u-%26-nintendo-3ds-eshop-discontinuation-q%26a

Nintendo Agonizes Over Price to Charge for Wii U. (2012). *The Nikkei Weekly (Japan)*. NexisUni.

Nintendo Continues Streak of Super Profits, Mulls Next Move. (2008). *The Nikkei Weekly (Japan)*. NexisUni.

Nintendo Creates New Game Plan. (2004). *The Nikkei Weekly (Japan)*. NexisUni.

Nintendo Crisis Casts Shadow on Famicom's 30th Anniversary. (2013). *The Nikkei Weekly (Japan)*. NexisUni.

Nintendo Easing Iron Grip on Programmers Video-Game Giant Halves Minimum Cartridge Order. (1994). *The Nikkei Weekly (Japan)*. NexisUni.

Nintendo Embarks on Major Sales Drive with Ambitious "DS for All" Target. (2009). *The Nikkei Weekly (Japan)*. NexisUni.

Nintendo Enjoys Healthy Profits, Yet Frets Over Japan Sales Slowdown. (2008). *The Nikkei Weekly (Japan)*. NexisUni.

Nintendo Expects Record Profit on Booming Consoles. (2007). *The Nikkei Weekly (Japan)*. NexisUni.

Nintendo Flush, But Growth Stalling. (2003). *The Nikkei Weekly (Japan)*. NexisUni.

Nintendo Gives Details on Wii. (2006). *The Nikkei Weekly (Japan)*. NexisUni.

Nintendo History. (2021). *Nintendo of Europe GmbH.* Retrieved June 9, 2021, from https://www.nintendo.co.uk/Corporate/Nintendo-History/Nintendo-History-625945.html

Nintendo Looks to 3-D Game Device to Spark Return to Earnings Fun. (2010). *The Nikkei Weekly (Japan).* NexisUni.

Nintendo Loses Its Visionary Chief. (2015). *Nikkei Asian Review (Japan).* NexisUni.

Nintendo Profit Rises on Handheld Consoles. (2006). *The Nikkei Weekly (Japan).* NexisUni.

Nintendo Profits Tumble 15%; Sega Reports 45% Plunge. (1995). *The Nikkei Weekly (Japan).* NexisUni.

Nintendo Readies Advanced Consoles. (2000). *The Nikkei Weekly (Japan).* NexisUni.

Nintendo Set to Ship 400,000 Wii Units. (2006). *The Nikkei Weekly (Japan).* NexisUni.

Nintendo Settles Lawsuits. (1994). *Consumer Electronics.* NexisUni.

Nintendo Starts 3 Europe Units. (1993). *The Nikkei Weekly (Japan).* NexisUni.

Nintendo Suit by Atari is Dismissed. (1992). *The New York Times.* NexisUni.

Nintendo Takes Off Gloves in Battle with Sony Price Cut Seen as Way to Catch PlayStation, Lure Game Designers. (1997). *The Nikkei Weekly (Japan).* NexisUni.

Nintendo to Make, Sell Games in China. (1993). *The Nikkei Weekly (Japan).* NexisUni.

Nintendo to Offer Cheaper Handheld in Europe, U.S. (2013). *The Nikkei Weekly (Japan).* NexisUni.

Nintendo to Sell 1.5 Million Shares Held by Major Shareholders. (1983). *Jiji Press English News Service.* NexisUni.

Nintendo to Sell Video Game Player-Robot Combination in U.S. (1985). *The Japan Economic Journal.* NexisUni.

Nintendo/Universal; U.S. Court of Appeals Affirms Dismissal of King Kong Trademark Infringement Suit. (1984). *Business Wire.* NexisUni.

Nintendo Urges Trade Action to End Video Game Piracy. (1996). *PR Newswire,* 220DCTU025.

Nintendo Uses Off-the-Shelf Tech, Flexibility to Outfox Rivals. (2008). *The Nikkei Weekly (Japan).* NexisUni.

Nintendo Wiki. (2023a). *Doug Bowser.* Nintendo Wiki. https://nintendo.fandom.com/wiki/Doug_Bowser

Nintendo Wiki. (2023b). *List of Nintendo People.* Nintendo Wiki. https://nintendo.fandom.com/wiki/List_of_Nintendo_people

Nintendo Wiki. (2023c). *Minoru Arakawa.* Nintendo Wiki. https://nintendo.fandom.com/wiki/Minoru_Arakawa

Nintendo Wiki. (2023d). *Nintendo of Korea.* Nintendo Wii. https://nintendo.fandom.com/wiki/St%C3%A9phan_Bole

Nintendo Wiki. (2023e). *Reggie Fils-Aimé.* Nintendo Wiki. https://nintendo.fandom.com/wiki/Reggie_Fils-Aim%C3%A9

Nintendo Wiki. (2023f). *Satoru Shibata.* Nintendo Wiki. https://nintendo.fandom.com/wiki/Satoru_Shibata

Nintendo Wiki. (2023g). *Stéphan Bole.* Nintendo Wii. https://nintendo.fandom.com/wiki/St%C3%A9phan_Bole

Nintendo Wiki. (2023h). *Tatsumi Kimishima.* Nintendo Wiki. https://nintendo.fandom.com/wiki/Tatsumi_Kimishima

Nintendo's Downsized, Low-Price Wii Heads into European Markets. (2013). *The Nikkei Weekly (Japan).* NexisUni.

Nintendo's Iwata Sizing Up M&As to Gain Technologies. (2007). *The Nikkei Weekly (Japan)*. NexisUni.

Nintendo's Profit Zooms Upward from Popularity of Its Electronic Games. (1982). *The Japan Economic Journal*. NexisUni.

Nintendo's Recurring Profit up 18.4 PCT. (1985). *Jiji Press English News Service*. NexisUni.

Oikawa, A. (2010). Nintendo's 3-D Cash Cow Can't Come Soon Enough. *The Nikkei Weekly (Japan)*. NexisUni.

Oikawa, A. (2011a). For Nintendo, Fun Hinges on Games. *The Nikkei Weekly (Japan)*. NexisUni.

Oikawa, A. (2011b). Nintendo's Profit, Sales Take Dive. *The Nikkei Weekly (Japan)*. NexisUni.

Oikawa, A. (2011c). Sweating in Super Mario Land. *The Nikkei Weekly (Japan)*. NexisUni.

Olenick, D. (1999). Dreamcast Has Registers Ringing. *TWICE, 14*(29), 68.

Pollack, A. (1996). Seeking a Turnaround with Souped-Up Machines and a Few New Games. *The New York Times*.

Popeye Ramen – NintendoWiki. (2019, October 15). https://niwanetwork.org/wiki/Popeye_Ramen

Portable Game Consoles Cheer Up Market. (2004). *The Nikkei Weekly (Japan)*. NexisUni.

Portable Game Players Trump Home Consoles. (2006). *The Nikkei Weekly (Japan)*. NexisUni.

Ramirez, A. (1990). Waiting for the Zapping of Nintendo. *The New York Times*. NexisUni.

Rene, S., Rhodes, N., Peippo, K., McNulty, M., & Lacoma, T. (2014). Nintendo Company, Ltd. *International Directory of Company Histories, 157*, 303–309.

Report: Top 10 Highest-Grossing Arcade Games of All Time. (2015, January 7). *Nintendo Enthusiast*. https://www.nintendoenthusiast.com/report-top-10-highest-grossing-games-time/

Ryan, J. (2011). *Super Mario: How Nintendo Conquered America*. New York: Portfolio Penguin.

Saijo, K. (2007). Nintendo's Non-Japanese Approach. *The Nikkei Weekly (Japan)*. NexisUni.

Sales of Video Games in Japan Topped One-Million Mark Last Year. (1984). *The Japan Economic Journal*. NexisUni.

Sese, S., & Oikawa, A. (2011). Nintendo Sticking to Familiar Markets with Next Wii Home Gaming Console. *The Nikkei Weekly (Japan)*. NexisUni.

Sharp Develops TV with Microcomputer. (1983). *The Japan Economic Journal*. NexisUni.

Sheff, D. (1993). *Game Over: How Nintendo Zapped an American Industry, Captured Your Dollars, and Enslaved Your Children*. New York, NY: Random House.

Shenzhen's Success Overshadows China's Other Special Economic Zones. (n.d.). *Nikkei Asia*. Retrieved September 6, 2021, from https://asia.nikkei.com/Economy/Shenzhen-s-success-overshadows-China-s-other-special-economic-zones

Simons, T. (1991). Nintendo Gives Coupons to Settle Price-Fixing Case. *United Press International*. NexisUni.

Sloan, D. (2011). *Playing to Wiin: Nintendo and the Video Game Industry's Greatest Comeback*. Singapore: Wiley Asia.

Slow-to-Adapt Nintendo Reeling in the Smartphone Era. (2014). *Nikkei Asian Review (Japan)*. NexisUni.

Steinberg, N. (2017, November 3). *The 25 Best-Selling Arcade Games of All Time*. Goliath. https://www.goliath.com/gaming/the-25-best-selling-arcade-games-of-all-time/

Suruga, T. (2017). Nintendo's Switch is Almost Too Popular for Its Own Good. *Nikkei Asian Review (Japan)*. NexisUni.

Sutherland, A. (2012). *The Story of Nintendo*. New York: Rosen Publishing Group.

Tsutsumi, M. (2009). Nintendo's Appeal Fades with Stamina in Doubt. *The Nikkei Weekly (Japan)*. NexisUni.

Unozawa, S. (2002). Nintendo Sees Generational Change. *The Nikkei Weekly (Japan)*. NexisUni.

VGChartz.com. (2023). Platform Totals. *VGChartz*. https://www.vgchartz.com

VGLegacy. (2023). Video Game Console Generations – VG Legacy | Hardware Platforms. *VG Legacy*. https://vglegacy.com/platforms/

Video Games Will be Made in U.S. (1981). *The Japan Economic Journal*. NexisUni.

Watanabe, J. (2012). Nintendo Ready to Change World of Gaming, again, with Wii U Console. *The Nikkei Weekly (Japan)*. NexisUni.

Watanabe, N. (2008a). Europe Tops North, South America in Nintendo Sales. *The Nikkei Weekly (Japan)*. NexisUni.

Watanabe, N. (2008b). Is Nintendo Jumping Gun with November Release of Revamped DS? *The Nikkei Weekly (Japan)*. NexisUni.

Watanabe, N. (2008c). Nintendo Taking DS Beyond Gaming, Into e-Book, Net Access. *The Nikkei Weekly (Japan)*. NexisUni.

Watanabe, N., & Hirooka, N. (2008). Nintendo Caught in Dilemma Over Next-Generation Console. *The Nikkei Weekly (Japan)*. NexisUni.

Welsh, O. (2017, February 24). A Complete History of Nintendo Console Launches. *Eurogamer*. https://www.eurogamer.net/articles/2017-02-24-a-complete-history-of-nintendo-console-launches

"Wii Delive" – Nintendo Plans Entry Into Video Delivery Market. (2009). *The Nikkei Weekly (Japan)*. NexisUni.

Yamazaki, A. (1997). U.S. Sales Put Nintendo Back in the Game Company's Results for Fiscal 1996 Better than Expected. *The Nikkei Weekly (Japan)*. NexisUni.

3   Nintendo's Economic
        Profile

Though Nintendo was founded at the end of the 19th century, its tenure as a media giant really begins in 1983, with the release of its first console, the Famicon/Ninendo Entertainment System (NES). While this wasn't the company's first foray into electronic games, it did mark the company's move into video games more specifically, and it quickly helped the company establish its dominance in a newly emerging industry. Indeed, many of the patterns that have allowed the company to be so successful were established early prior to its entrance into the video game market. This chapter draws on the history of the company established in Chapter 2 to help better understand the company's economic profile, including strategies in dealing with both manufacturing and labor. In addition, it examines the structure of the company and its board of directors to provide some understanding of the company's decisions and likely future directions.

Red Ocean, Blue Ocean – Nintendo's
Two Primary Markets

Recent business literature has emphasized Nintendo as taking a "blue ocean" strategy in business, particularly during the introduction of the Wii (Hollensen, 2013). Blue ocean strategy is one half of a metaphor conceived of by Mauborgne and Kim (2005). According to this metaphor, a company might work in either a "red ocean" – in which markets, competitors, and consumers are all well-defined and, so, the competition is fierce – or in a blue ocean – in which all of those factors are still able to be defined or capable of being defined by the firm itself. Put another way, the blue ocean is one in which there isn't such fierce competition because things like price, quality, and service haven't yet been normalized.

Though the company was already an industry powerhouse by the time the Wii console was introduced, Hollensen (2013) argues that Nintendo's launch of the console represented a radical shift in how the company thought about games. This is a point that Jones and Thiruvathukal (2012) also emphasized, noting that the Wii (and later, the Wii U) marked a distinctive change in video

DOI: 10.4324/9781003031918-3

games and in Nintendo's thinking. There is even some evidence that this thinking was mirrored by consumers (Shay and Palomba, 2020). It is also worth considering the role of marketing in creating the sense that such changes are, in fact, sea shifts (Wesley and Barczak, 2010). Part of this thinking rests on the idea that the core business of Nintendo and its chief competitors in the video game industry, Sony and Microsoft, is the console. As such, innovations in consoles represent sea changes in the industry.

But this ignores one key fact: all three of the firms which dominate the console sector of the industry – Nintendo, Microsoft, and Sony – have sold their consoles at a loss, emphasizing the importance of software sales as a mechanism to make money. Consoles aren't their primary source of profit; software is. All three companies have tended to operate at a loss for a year or more after the introduction of new hardware, counting on the revenue from software to keep them profitable (Nichols, 2014). This has been a long-standing logic of the video game industry, all the way back to Nintendo's introduction of the Famicom/NES in the early 1980s. And while the blue ocean metaphor emphasizes a seeking of new audiences, something Nintendo certainly emphasized with the Wii, seeking new audiences was not, as Chapter 2 demonstrated, a new goal for the company. Thus, without a more detailed study of the video game industry's logics of production, it becomes very difficult to accurately assess how any company or product actually fits in to the strategy.

Logics of Production in the Video Game Industry

As Bernard Miege (1987, 1989a, 1989b) notes, every cultural industry organizes itself around a particular set of norms and practices around production. He terms these "logics of production," and they help to make sense of the ways in which production attempts to address how production relates to audiences/ consumers, how companies relate within themselves and between themselves and other institutions, and even how the State might have an impact on production. These logics are as much active choices, such as the particular choices and strategies that might result in a red or blue ocean, as they are results of a range of outside factors. How those logics both shape what markets exist for the industry and how they function is historically contingent, with a change in one feature resulting in changes in some or all of the others (Nichols, 2014). Adherence to or deviation from those logics creates alternate pathways. One example of such a deviation is independent game production. A second is how the change to digital distribution and mobile technologies has resulted in changes to industry structure (Kerr, 2017).

Since the video game industry stabilized in the late 1980s and early 1990s, the mainstream video game industry (as opposed to independent game production) has followed the same general set of logics and existed with a relatively stable structure (Nichols, 2014). First, the industry has sought to ensure long-term demand by cultivating long-term audiences. In some cases, this has been through the careful deployment of beloved brands as well as the cultivation of a set of values associated with those brands. Second, make use of planned obsolescence to drive demand and to prompt innovation. This has been particularly crucial in the hardware sector of the industry, but it has had significant impact on the software side as well. Third, plan production to take advantage of major buying seasons, particularly the holiday season and summer. Fourth, keep production costs down as a way to minimize risk (Nichols, 2014). As Chapter 1 notes, nearly all of these are practices that Nintendo undertook from its first days of entering into the video game industry. Having that basic understanding of how Nintendo and the mainstream video game industry have tended to work, it is easier to understand both Nintendo's specific position within that industry and how it wields its power and influence.

But it is also necessary to understand how the industry itself is structured to better understand Nintendo's role. Briefly, the industry has stabilized into four sectors: hardware production, software distribution, software development, and retail (Nichols, 2013, 2014). Hardware production involves all the businesses, firms, and labor needed to manufacture the machines that video games are played on. Typically, this has been discussed in terms of consoles and handhelds, but as new players have entered the industry, mobile phones and tablets have taken on increasing importance as well. Software distribution represents the part of the industry involved in getting video game software – the games themselves – onto hardware platforms and into retail spaces. As is the case with many media industries, control of distribution has proved to be a particularly crucial sector. Software development includes all the work and labor involved in creating the video games themselves, including programming, art, music, quality assurance, licensing, marketing, and a range of other duties (Ruggill et al., 2016). Finally, retail involves all the ways in which games are sold. Through the early 21st century, that meant retail stores, but the rise of digital distribution has changed that, fundamentally altering the industry.

Through roughly 2010, the games industry was dominated by four to five major companies, three of whom were involved in both hardware production and software distribution (Nichols, 2014). At that time, digital distribution and mobile games became a key feature, opening up the market to a variety of businesses. Up until 2010, digital distribution was largely seen as a way for the major console manufacturers – Nintendo, Sony, and Microsoft – to extend the lifecycle of their consoles, with each company developing both digital stores to sell software and, in some cases, digital subscription services (Stelter, 2010). However, the reality has been that it has opened up the games industry to new forms of competition, though the major new competitors are largely other global giants. Table 3.1 details the top ten companies by revenue in 2020. The table shows a number of important things about the video industry, most notably the volatility that still exists among the second-tier companies, which move in and out of top positions based largely on sales of a hit software product. For Nintendo, it also marks a rare moment where the company wasn't in the top ten, because of poor sales both of its more recent consoles and the software for it. The launch of the Nintendo Switch just a few years later would quickly vault

Table 3.1 Top Ten Video Game Companies Globally by Revenue, 2015 and 2020 in Billions of U.S. Dollars

2015		2020	
Tencent	$8.7	Tencent	$8.25
Microsoft	$6.8	Sony	$4.33
Sony	$5.8	Apple	$3.49
Activision Blizzard	$4.7	Microsoft	$3.08
Apple	$4.4	NetEase	$2.72
Electronic Arts	$4.3	Google	$2.44
Google	$3.0	Nintendo	$1.84
NetEase	$2.8	Electronic Arts	$1.83
Warner Bros.	$2.2	Activision Blizzard	$1.67
King	$2.0	Bandai Namco Entertainment	$1.21

Source: (Newzoo, 2016; Newzoo, 2022)

the company back into top position. It also provides some clear evidence of the growing importance of both the Chinese market, represented by both Tencent and NetEase, as well as the increasing importance of digital distribution. The shift to digital distribution is tied to another crucial development: the use of smart phones as digital devices. This not only has proved particularly important for companies like Apple and Google, as they have entered the games field, but also has been central to Tencent's rise (Tang, 2019; Tedesco, 2009).

Financial Performance and Market Share

In 2020, global video games software was worth between $159 billion and $179 billion and was projected to reach almost $220 billion by 2023 (Wijman, 2020a, 2020b; Witkowski, 2021). Fueled in part by the need for entertainment during the global pandemic, that amount was more than the global movie box office and North American sports industries combined. During this period, hardware sales rose worldwide by 34 percent, earning the industry nearly $4 billion, though this amount was felt primarily in the North American market (Witkowski, 2021).

As a company, Nintendo has been highly profitable, even at times of economic downturn for the industry, and the pandemic was no different. As seen in Chapter 2, the company's core business became video games starting in the 1980s, and it has remained a key player since that shift. In 2020, Nintendo reported sales of $12.1 billion and profit of over $3 billion (Nintendo, 2020). That gave Nintendo roughly a 10 percent share of the global games market, down from almost 18 percent in 2015 (Euromonitor International, 2021). Table 3.2 details Nintendo's historical market share globally and in key markets from 2011 to 2020. Key to the company's decline has been the entrance of new competitors like Apple, Amazon, Google, and Tencent into the video game market.

Table 3.2 Global Market Share of the Video Game Industry by Company, 2018

	Revenue in Millions of U.S. Dollars	*Percentage of Global Market*
Tencent Holdings Ltd.	$19,733.00	17.31
Sony Corp.	14,218.00	12.47
Microsoft Corp.	9,754.00	8.56
Apple Inc.	9,453.00	8.29
Activision Blizzard Inc.	6,892.00	6.05
Google Inc.	6,497.00	5.70
NetEase Inc.	6,177.00	5.42
Electronic Arts Inc.	5,294.00	4.64
Nintendo Co. Ltd.	4,288.00	3.76

Source: (Burton and Lazich, 2021; Euromonitor, 2021)

However, as even a cursory review of the financial reporting on Nintendo reveals, the company continues to navigate cycles of boom and bust. These cycles are typically tied to the release of new consoles and the success of the software for those consoles. Figure 3.1 shows Nintendo's sales from 2001 to 2020. While the boom-and-bust trend is clear on its own, the highlighted data indicates sales response following years of key console releases. The success or failure of each console, and more importantly the software for that console, is the clearest predictor of the company's successes. The three dates marked by their associated net sales are for the fiscal years following the release of the Wii, Wii U, and Switch consoles. As has been discussed the Wii and Switch were both seen as tremendous successes for Nintendo, while the Wii U is widely regarded as a failure. Though the company has maintained support for other consoles even as it released new ones, how well a new console and its software perform is crucial for the success of the company.

The Hardware Sector

Perhaps the most visible sector that Nintendo operates in is in video games consoles, which has often been discussed as one of two segments of the games hardware market: consoles and handhelds (Nichols, 2014). Nintendo has been active in both segments, frequently achieving a near monopoly in the handheld segment. As Table 3.3 shows, by 2021, not only was the Nintendo Switch the only handheld console in the market, its sales dwarfed those of the two most recent handheld consoles in the market. That is made all the more impressive since one of the two discontinued handhelds was also manufactured by Nintendo. However, as the rise of smart phones has allowed new players into the video game industry, it also marks a distinctly new sector of hardware.

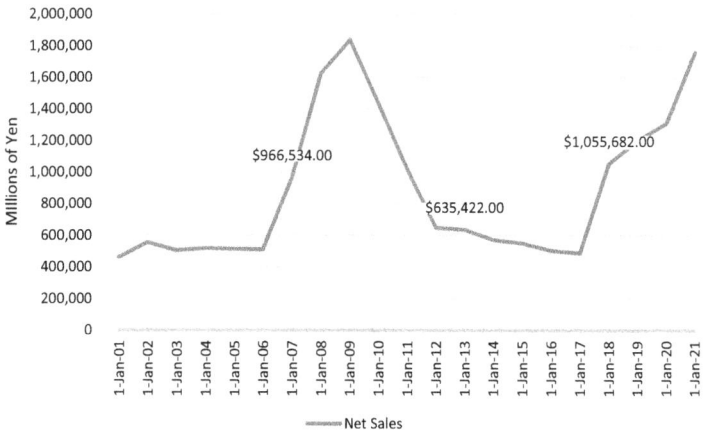

Figure 3.1 Nintendo Co. Ltd. Net Sales, 2001–2020

Source: (Nintendo, 2003, 2004, 2005, 2006, 2007, 2008, 2009, 2010, 2011, 2012, 2013, 2014, 2015, 2016, 2017, 2018, 2019, 2020, 2021, 2022a)

Table 3.3 U.S. Sales of Video Game Consoles and Handhelds, 2021

Console	Millions of Units Sold	Platform Type
Nintendo Switch	114.31	Handheld
Sony PlayStation 5	24.98	Console
Xbox X	17.7	Console
Nintendo 3DS (discontinued September 2020)	75.94	Handheld
PlayStation Vita (discontinued March 2019)	15.82	Handheld

Source: (Burton, 2023; VGChartz.com, 2022f)

For much of the industry's history, there were three markets that were emphasized: the North American market, the Japanese market, and the European market. As Chapter 2 details, Nintendo has periodically shifted its emphasis on these markets. One way the importance of a market could be seen was in the release date. In the company's early years, the Japanese market received consoles first, followed by the North American market. In some cases, the European market did not see console releases until a year or more after the console reached the other two. Eventually, the North American market was seen as the most fertile, with release dates reflecting this. But increasingly, Nintendo has also recognized the importance of other global markets for the company's continued success. Figure 3.2 provides a breakdown of console sales across different groupings of global markets. It clearly indicates the growing importance of both the European market and sales in the rest of the world. Sales of consoles

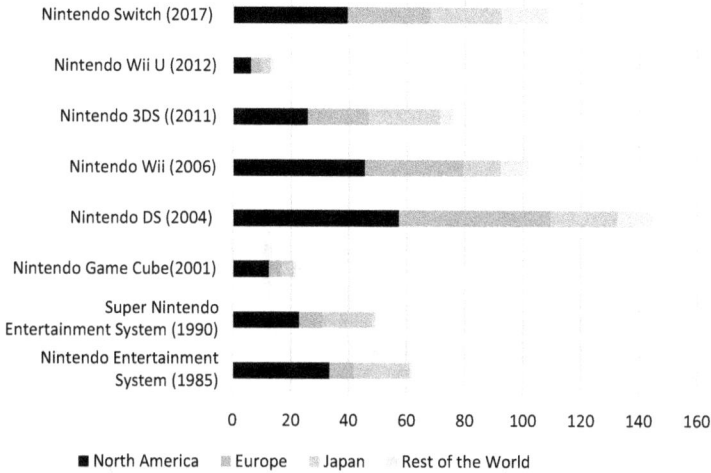

Figure 3.2 Global Console Sales of Nintendo Platform by Region
Source: (VGChartz.com, 2022g)

released since 2004 have relied more heavily on both the European market, and those since 2006 – particularly the Wii and the Switch – have owed much of their success to sales from other parts of the globe.

The Software Sector

As discussed, Nintendo's continued dominance in the market would not be possible without its place in the software sector. The company functions primarily as a software publisher, distributing games for its various platforms. While the company engages in software development as well, the bulk of development for the company is handled by outside firms. This will be discussed further in this chapter in relation to the company's labor practices. To help ensure the company's position and reputation, Nintendo has from its earliest days in the video game industry used highly restrictive contracts with software developers (Nichols, 2014). In turn, as discussed in Chapter 2, these arrangements set many of the norms for the industry.

As a result of this and its platforms' popularity, Nintendo has had an unusually successful track record in producing successful selling software titles. Figure 3.3 shows the number of best-selling titles by company for the five-year period from 2013 to 2018. Notably, Nintendo has been one of a small number of companies making it into the yearly rankings of best-selling titles. Only two other companies – Electronic Arts and Activision Blizzard – also consistently

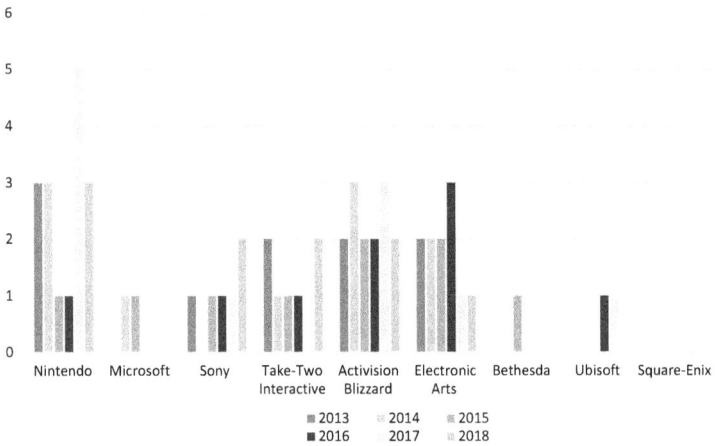

Figure 3.3 Number of Top Ten Best-Selling Software Titles Globally by Publisher
Source: (VGChartz.com, 2022a, 2022b, 2022c, 2022d, 2022e)

had software titles in each year, though neither totaled as many best-selling titles in that period. As seen earlier in this chapter, even in years such as 2015 where the company struggled in terms of overall global sales, the company was able to buoy itself with successful software sales.

Unlike many of the companies it competes with in both the hardware and software sectors – particularly the other console manufacturers – Nintendo has no additional businesses to offset the volatility of the video game sectors. From its earliest days, the company has been both solely focused on entertainment and mindful of the risks posed by working exclusively in that area. Because of this, it has developed a variety of strategies in terms of how it approaches product development, costs of production, labor, and managing its finances.

Strategies

Even as Nintendo has been somewhat resistant to some aspects of the digital shifts in the video game industry, particularly mobile gaming, it continues to act as a crucial gatekeeper and trendsetter across the industry, along with Sony and Microsoft (Kerr, 2017). Because the company views the industry as particularly precarious, much of the strategies it has adopted are measures to minimize production costs and to ensure the possibility of significant cash flow for periods of economic downturn.

Outsourcing and Licensing

One key component to Nintendo's success has been its use of outsourcing and licensing (Harding, 2008). While the company is often discussed in terms of its hardware, the bulk of the work done within the company is conceptual and developmental. For hardware this means developing the concept and proto-types of the consoles, then outsourcing the majority of the production. This is not unusual in high-tech industries, particularly video games, in which a major-ity of hardware production is the result of a large and intensely globalized sup-ply chain (Nichols, 2013). What is noteworthy, however, is how few of its own production facilities the company owns (Nintendo, 2021). One benefit of this production model is that it makes it more difficult to track and, thus, link prob-lematic production practices back to any given company. In particular, labor and environmental issues become much harder to track (Nichols, 2013). The company is particularly shrewd in its outsourcing and licensing deals, requir-ing exclusive contracts whenever possible. In some cases, this has meant the company avoided awarding production contracts in particular regions because it viewed the deals as unfavorable ("Japanese TV Game . . .," 1982). By empha-sizing the need for such favorable conditions for the company in every con-tract, particularly through long term, exclusive contracts with producers has the potential to give the company some degree of monopsony power in its interactions.

Until 2019, Nintendo assembled most of its consoles in China, working with the Foxconn, the same company known for the manufacturing of Apple iPhones; more recently it has shifted some of its manufacture to Vietnam (Shen, 2020). But as with other consoles, the manufacture relies on a range of supplies including rare minerals and plastics to be assembled into the component parts, many of which come from areas of intense global conflict (Nichols, 2013). The materials for microchips and touch screens, in particular, have frequently caused supply chain issues for Nintendo and other companies. The Switch, for example, experienced significant delays during the height of the pandemic, slowing down the console's record sales (Eshkenazi, 2017; Mochizuki, 2022). Microchips, in particular, were central to this logjam, impacting all three major console manufacturers, though each has had its own strategy for developing and procuring microchips (Tomaselli et al., 2008; Wong, 2022).

This globalized chain of production effectively externalizes much of the risk to workers' health as well as environmental impacts, largely placing them in the Global South despite a majority of hardware sales occurring in North America, western Europe, and parts of Asia (Lam, 2019). The labor required for this work has received little attention, though it is clear that the consequences can be particularly dire for those involved, while the compensation received makes access to the very products being produced nearly impossible for anyone build-ing them (Nichols, 2013). Nintendo has attempted to address many of these concerns under the banner of corporate social responsibility, bringing in specific guidelines for its procurement of parts and resources and outlining guidelines for how it vets potential production partners. In addition, the company has begun to work with outside auditors to review its supply chain for outstanding issues (Nintendo, 2022d). Some concern has been raised, as well, because of the power major producers have to influence smaller companies they are purchasing from (Kumar, 2020; Maxwell and Miller, 2012). These issues are taken up again in Chapter 4.

Software development, too, is heavily done through outsourced licensed work (Weber, 2017). Nintendo has long led the way for the industry in this regard, with many concepts developed in-house, including games tied to the company's key franchises (Harding, 2008). A central feature of its licensing deals with software developers have been deals granting Nintendo both exclusive rights to a game and the final decision on whether a game is published or not (Counsell, 1992). Under such an arrangement, a developer might find themselves working for more than a year on a particular game, only to have Nintendo determine that it will not be published but also that the developer could not adjust the game to be sold on a rival platform. And given that these contracts also typically left much of the costs of making software in the hands of developers, these contracts were particularly favorable for Nintendo and potentially devastating for any development team whose work wasn't given the green light (Nichols, 2014; Sloan, 2011). The importance of these contractual arrangements for the company is clear, given how important revenue from licensed games has been to the company (Ishizawa, 1992).

Intellectual Property Deployment and Control

Nintendo's deployment of its intellectual property (IP) is a particularly fascinating area. As discussed in Chapter 4, Nintendo owns some of the most recognizable IP in the world, so perhaps because much of it is so family friendly, the company has been frequently compared to Disney (Lewis and Inagaki, 2020). And yet, it would seem that Nintendo has been more hesitant to take advantage of its IP beyond its redeployment in video games (Quast et al., 2021). Such hesitancy is consistent with the company's historical tendencies, discussed in Chapter 2, in licensing for game development, in which any game which didn't meet the company's standards was shelved entirely (Counsell, 1992).

That would change following the success of the Switch, the Covid pandemic, and the company's struggles following the Wii U. Its first notable foray was the creation of the mobile game *Pokémon Go* in 2016 by company Niantic, a game developer, Nintendo and Google each own undisclosed stakes in. The game, only the second venture into mobile gaming by the company, was created after Nintendo investors outlined the importance of the mobile platform. The game's announcement initially sent the company's stock soaring (Choudhury,

2016; Nichols, 2020). Nintendo's next move was the creation of Super Nintendo World, a theme park within many of NBCUniversal's Universal Studios theme parks, that will take advantage of the company's IP library. The first such park was scheduled to open in Osaka, Japan in the summer of 2020, with similar parks planned for Universal Studios Hollywood, Orlando, and Singapore parks in the coming years. The company has also partnered with Illumination, an animation studio, to make an animated movie based on its IP, going so far as bringing the head of the studio in as an outside board member (Lewis and Inagaki, 2020; "Illumination Boss . . .," 2021). That film scheduled to be released in 2023, *The Super Mario Bros. Movie*, was seen as the first step to expanding the company's efforts to extend its connection with fans beyond its games (Kageyama, 2022). Finally, in July 2022 Nintendo announced its intention to create its own movie studio, purchasing Dynamo Pictures, a company focused on CGI productions, with the intention of renaming it Nintendo Pictures. The company has previous games-to-movie experience having worked on the Final Fantasy franchise of films among other projects (Tedder, 2022).

In keeping with the company's concerns over IP noted earlier, Nintendo has built a reputation for litigation and has experienced its share of notable suits. In the company's early years in the video game industry, it was more prone to being sued than to suing. The 1981 arcade hit *Donkey Kong*, resulted in the company being sued by Universal Studios on grounds of infringement on Universal's King Kong property (Barnes, 2021). Rival Atari sued the company in 1989 for monopoly practices over the terms of its development contracts (Associated Press, 1989). Nintendo would win both lawsuits, but it was far from the end of the company's time in court. The same year of the Atari lawsuit, Nintendo's first notable suit against another company was launched, with the company unsuccessfully suing Blockbuster Video. While the company was fearful of the renting of video games, since they would get no royalty, the suit invoked copyright violations over Blockbuster's practice of reproducing copies of game manuals for any rentals in which they'd been lost (Chan, 2021).

Unsurprisingly, copyright and patent infringement has become a key theme to litigation for Nintendo. Since its Blockbuster lawsuit, the company has been involved in frequent litigation over fan created games and mods (modifications to a game that alter the way it works or is interacted with), films, trailers, and tournaments (Chan, 2021; Barnes, 2021). More recently, the company has been heavily involved in suits over piracy, in which games have been made available over ROM sites – function like more advanced versions of file sharing sites that plagued the movie and music industries in the early 21st century – some of which have charged users fees for access or better download rates. ROM sites (Carpenter, 2021).

Finally, the company's more recent successes, the Wii and the Switch, have both resulted in a number of lawsuits, most of which have been dismissed but a few of which ended in settlement. In the case of the Wii, the bulk of the lawsuits centered on patent issues surrounding the console's controller, which used motion tracking technology. That feature, considered highly innovative and a big part of the argument for the blue wave strategy discussed previously, resulted in several lawsuits from a variety of companies (Bae, 2022). In contrast, the Nintendo Switch was plagued a problem with its JoyCon controllers that caused it to falsely register some input and referred to as "Joy-Con Drift." While the problem was noted soon after the console's release, satisfactory fixes languished and by 2021, lawsuits were filed in a number of countries, though most were successfully resolved through arbitration (Sirani, 2021).

Component Costs

As discussed previously, one of the key logics of the video game industry is planned obsolescence of its technologies, which serves as a way to drive innovation. This is particularly apparent in the typical reliance within the industry on upgrading the capability of its microchips' processing power. This continuous upgrading of processing power is central to defining the various generations of hardware consoles (Nichols, 2013, 2014). While Nintendo, too, relies on planned obsolescence of its consoles, which typically follow the same three-to-five-year replacement cycle that other companies do, there is one crucial difference. Unlike the other major hardware manufacturers in the industry, Nintendo is less likely to attempt to develop entirely new technologies but rather seeks to use readily available technologies in novel ways as a means to keep its costs down and to avoid some of the supply chain issues that often beset other high-tech manufacturers (Saijo, 2007).

Perhaps the best example of this can be seen in the development of the controller for the Wii hardware platform. Called the Wii Remote, the controller consisted of both motion sensing and optical sensors that allowed users to control games through gestures, motions, and pointing. It was seen as quite innovative and was central in the sense that the Wii was a game-changing console for the industry (Wales, 2006; ESA, 2006; Hollensen, 2013; Wesley and Barczak, 2010). The remote was particularly successful, selling more than 8.5 million units in the United States in 2007 alone (Boyer, 2008). But what is most impressive is that many of the components for the controller were off the shelf, driving costs down ("Interview: Forsaking . . .," 2006). For example, as noted, the microchips which controlled much of the Wii's functionality cost only a few hundred yen at the time, a number much cheaper than the specialty chips developed for rival consoles from Microsoft and Sony (Saijo, 2007).

Innovative as it was, the practice of using lower cost components had long been a part of the company's strategy. As discussed in the previous chapter, this could be seen with the Game and Watch and with the N64. The former relied on relatively cheap watch batteries for power and basic LCDs, while the latter drew on an affordable microchip set (Sloan, 2011; Ryan, 2011). That practice is particularly important, as consoles typically are used as loss leaders. The more recent example of the Nintendo Switch is telling. Estimates suggest that the total cost of manufacture is roughly U.S. $257, with most of the cost being the Joy-Con controllers rather than the chips for the console and display. At that price point, it would leave the company only about U.S. $42 as potential profit for each unit sold (Hall, 2017).

Cash Reserves

Owing to the company's concerns about risk in the entertainment business, one crucial distinction has been the company's focus on maintain cash reserves. As discussed in Chapter 2, the company has long maintained a policy of keeping sufficient cash on hand to help the company continue through a number of years of economic downturn. In the 1990s, when the company was still managed by Yamauchi, it was noted that the company preferred to keep sufficient reserves on hand to cover costs – particularly employment costs – for at least three years (Mizuno,1993). Such reserves also allowed the company to be more selective in its outside borrowing, which it has done only selectively ("Company Complex . . .," 1996). At the height of the Wii success in 2008, it was estimated that the company had cash reserves in excess of a trillion yen ("Nintendo Continues . . .," 2008).

That reliance on cash reserves continues to be a feature of Nintendo's strategy. As Figure 3.4 shows, from 2015 to 2022, the company has continued to build sizable cash reserves in the boom years, while relying heavily on them during more troubled times. Following the failures of the Wii U in 2012 and

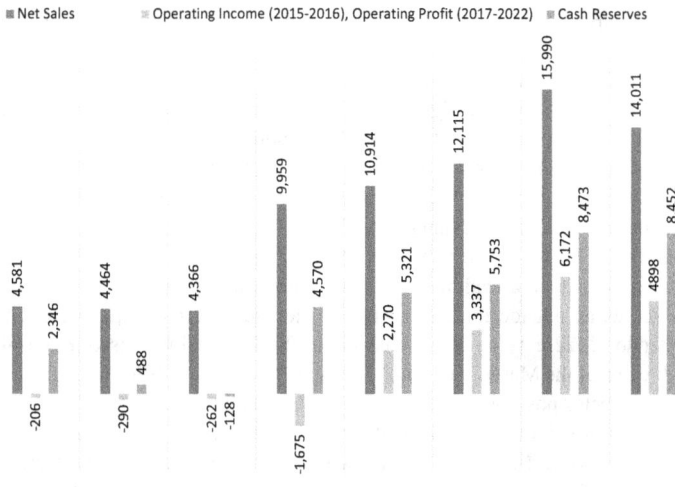

Figure 3.4 Comparison of Nintendo Financials with Cash Reserves, 2015–2022

All figures in millions of U.S. Dollars

Source: (Nintendo, 2015, 2016, 2017, 2018, 2019, 2020, 2021, 2022a)

the eventual ending of support for the Wii itself, the company had to draw more and more from its cash reserves, nearly depleting them in 2017. Fortunately, the launch and amazing success of the Switch platform, starting in that same year, allowed the company to replenish its reserves and build them further.

Corporate Structure

While the company has done some restructuring in the past, its general organization has changed relatively little. As Chapter 2 notes, for much of the company's history, it was essentially a family run corporation. The first major restructuring of the company took place when Hiroshi Yamauchi stepped down as president in 2002 ("Long-time Nintendo . . .," 2002). At that time the board increased its membership from four to six members, notably adding famed designer Shigeru Miyamoto as one of its new members (Unozawa, 2002; DeWinter, 2015).

Since then, the company has changed presidents several times, and as it has done so, it has continued to restructure. Figure 3.5 Shows the most recent restructuring which occurred between 2015 and 2017. That resulted in the company being divided into ten divisions, a majority of which are focused on product development in one form or another, with the remaining emphasizing the business and financial operations of the company (Rad and Otero, 2017). Each major division was headed by a then-member of the board, though some members oversaw more than one division.

Since that restructuring, the board has consisted of ten members, four of whom are from outside the company, a significant difference from Yamauchi's time when the board was much smaller ("Long-time Nintendo . . .", 2002; Nintendo, 2015, 2022a). Unsurprisingly, since that time, the composition of Nintendo's board has changed significantly, with a number of new members being added. Figure 3.6 shows the structure of Nintendo's Board of Directors in 2022. Among the outside directors are Chris Meledandri, the CEO of Illumination animation studio, who previously served at 20th Century Fox Animation ("Illumination Boss . . .," 2021; Nintendo, 2022b). In addition, other outside directors include the founder of the Umeyama Accounting Firm, Katsuhiro Umeyama, and Asa Shinkawa, a leading lawyer and partner at Nishimura & Asahi, who also serves as outside director at Tokyo Electric Power Company Holdings (Nintendo, 2022b: WSJ, 2022; Nishimura, 2022). Finally, Masao Yamazaki, the director of the Masao Yamazaki Certified Tax Account Office filled the final outside director position (Nintendo, 2022b; Nintendo Observer, 2022).

What those charts don't account for is the company's various subsidiaries around the world. Many of those companies represent particular markets the company is focused on. Table 3.4 details Nintendo's various wholly owned subsidiaries around the world, their local headquarters, and when possible, the person who oversees that part of the operation. As the table indicates, the company's expansion has come in waves, with significant gaming markets like

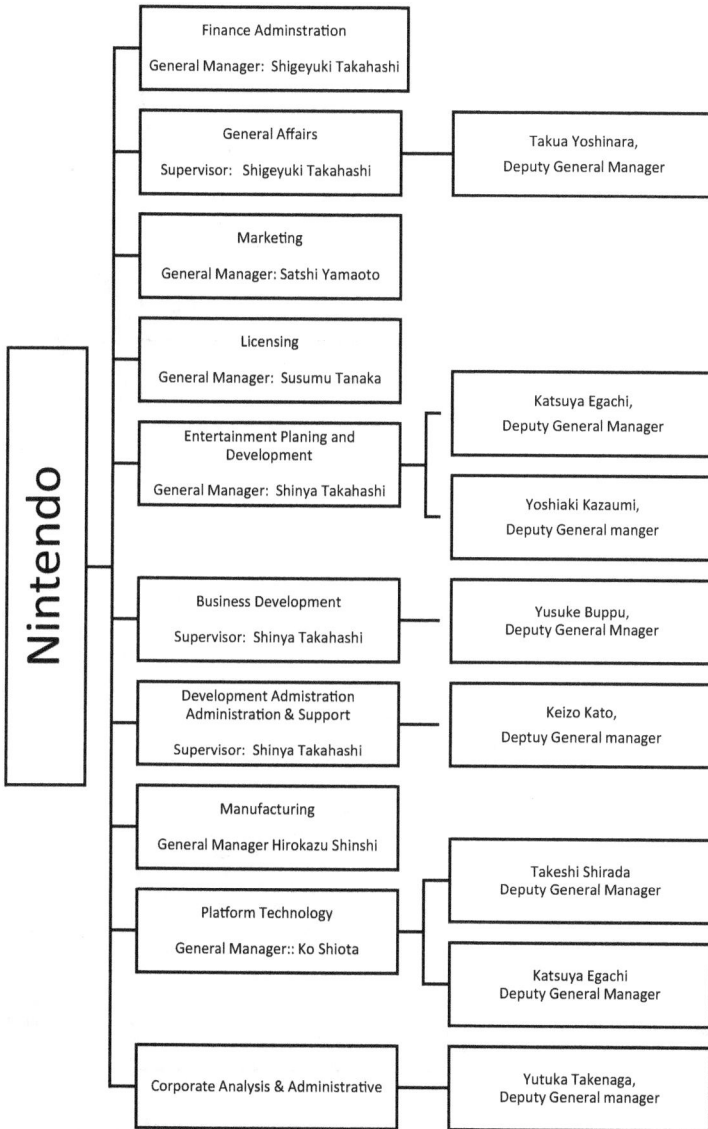

Figure 3.5 Nintendo Corporate Structure, 2017
Source: (Rad and Otero, 2017)

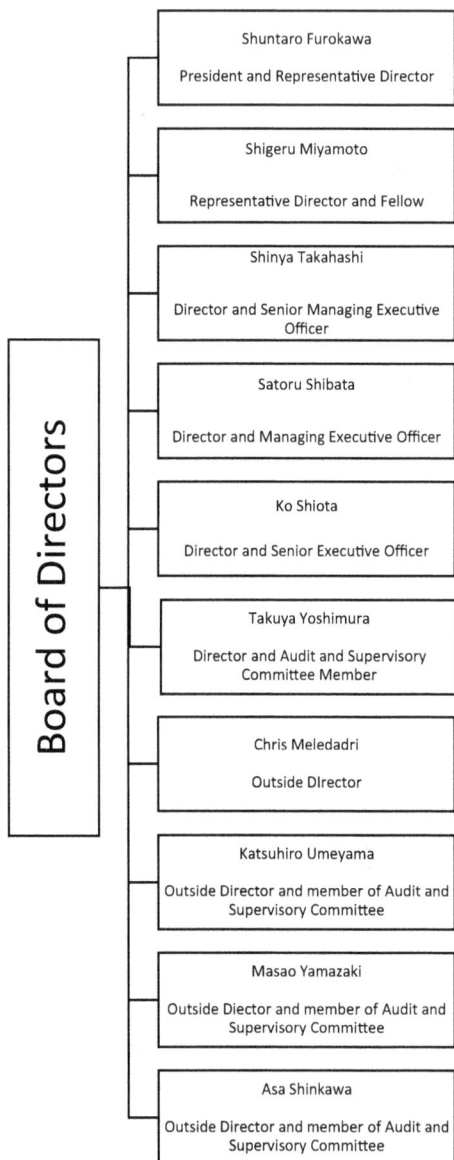

Figure 3.6 Nintendo Board of Directors, 2022

Source: (Nintendo, 2022b)

Table 3.4 Nintendo Global Subsidiaries, 2022

Subsidiary Name and Year Founded	Headquarters	Key People	Chief Function
Nintendo of America, Inc. (1980)	Redmond, WA, USA	Doug Bowser	Sales
Nintendo of Canada, Ltd. (1983)	Vancouver, Canada	Susan Pennefather	Sales
Nintendo of Europe, GMbH (1990)	Frankfurt am Main, Germany	Satoru Shibata	Sales
Nintendo France S.A.R.I. (1993)	Courbevoie, France	Stéphan Bole	Sales
Nintendo Benelux B.V. (1993)	Nieuwegein, The Netherlands	Stéphan Bole	Sales
Nintendo Ibérica S.A. (1993)	Madrid, Spain	Stéphan Bole	Sales
Nintendo RU LLC (2012)	Moscow, Russian Federation	Yasha Haddaji	Sales
Nintendo Australia Pty Limited (1993)	Scoresby, Australia	Takuro Horie	Sales
Nintendo of Korea Co. Ltd. (2006)	Seoul, Korea	Takahiro Miura	Sales
Nintendo (Hong Kong) Limited (2005)	Hong Kong	Mineichi Nonaka	Sales
Nintendo Technology Development Inc. (2015)	Kyoto, Japan	Ko Shiota	Development
Nintendo Software Technology Corporation (1998)	Redmond, WA, USA	Tim Bechtel	Development
Retro Studios Inc. (1998)	Austin, TX, USA	Michael Kelbaugh	Development
Next Level Games Inc. (2002)	Vancouver, Canada	Douglas Tronsgard	Development
Nintendo European Research and Development SAS (2003)	Paris, France	Alexandre Delattre	Development
iQue (China) Ltd. (2002)	Suzhou, China	Wei Yen	Development
Nintendo Sales Co., Ltd. (1952)	Kyoto, Japan	Satoshi Yamato	Sales
ND CUBE Co, Ltd (2000)	Tokyo, Japan	Shuichiro Nishiya	Development
1-Up Studio Inc. (2000)	Tokyo, Japan	Gen Kado	Development
MONOLITH SOFTWARE INC. (1999)	Tokyo, Japan	Hirohide Sugiura	Development
Mario Club Co., Ltd. (2009)	Kyoto, Japan	Unknown	Development

Source: (Nintendo, 2022a, 2022c)

Table 3.5 Jointly Owned Nintendo Ventures, 2022

Subsidiary Name and Year Founded	Headquarters	Percentage of Voting Rights Held by Nintendo	Partners	Chief Function
The Pokémon Company	Tokyo, Japan	32	Game Freak Creatures	Sale and licensing of Pokémon products
WARPSTAR, Inc.	Tokyo, Japan	50	HAL Laboratory, Inc.	Animation production and IP management
PUX Corporation	Osaka, Japan	27	MORPHO, Inc. Panasonic Holdings Corporation	Software engine and licensing

Source: (Nintendo, 2022a; MarketScreener, 2019; Whitehead, 2013)

Europe and Korea getting dedicated sales offices much later than parts of North America. The function of those subsidiaries has largely focused on three areas: sales of Nintendo consoles and hardware in particular regions, development of software, and development of new technologies and hardware.

Nintendo is also involved in several joint ventures. These joint ventures are detailed in Table 3.5. All three of these companies are centered in Japan. Two of the three have focused on expanding two jointly owned franchises – Pokémon and Kirby – as well as extending the company's reach in both software and anime. As will be discussed later in this chapter, these moves represent some of Nintendo's primary pushes toward diversification.

But it is also worth noting what isn't represented in either the company's wholly owned subsidiaries or its joint ventures is any clear presence in Central or South America, in any African nation, or in significant parts of Asia.

Labor Practices

Nintendo has traditionally operated as a very lean company, with a small number of employees relative to its product output and profits. Figure 3.7 shows a historical comparison of Nintendo and its major competitors within the industry. It clearly indicates just how lean the company has been, often employing fewer people than even companies focused primarily on software development and distribution like Electronic Arts and Activision Blizzard. But it also shows a recent uptick in employment for the company, which likely owes to the success of the Nintendo Switch as well as the company's moves to integrate.

The company's size reflects a particularly interesting system of valuation which emphasizes employee productivity as a key marker of corporate

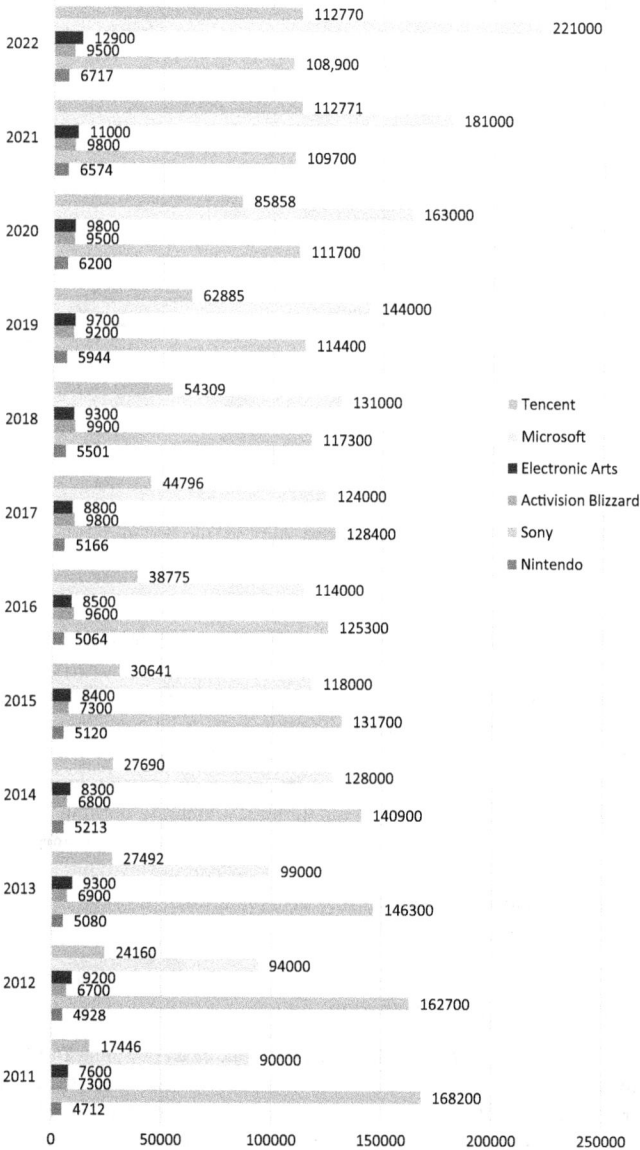

Figure 3.7 Number of Employees by Company in the Video Game Industry, 2011–2022

Source: (Macrotrends.com, 2022a, 2022b, 2022c; Nintendo, 2015, 2019, 2020, 2021, 2022a; Statista, 2022a, 2022b; TradingEconomics.com, 2022; Zippia, 2022)

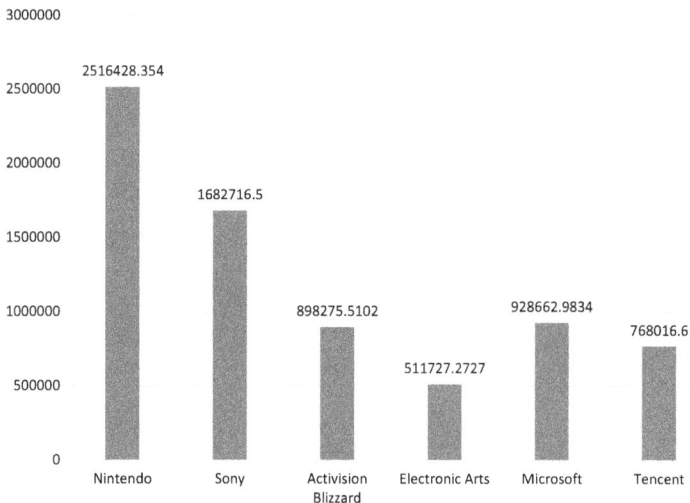

Figure 3.8 Nintendo's Revenue per Employee, 2021, in U.S. Dollars

Source: Macrotrends.com 2022a, 2022b, 2022c; Marketcap.com 2022a, 2022b, 2022c, 2022d, 2022e, 2022f

success and profitability. This valuation seeks to understand how much profit the company earns per employee. As seen in Figure 3.8, Nintendo's revenue per employee for fiscal year 2021, the company's lean employment has not been detrimental to its successes. According to this metric, the company easily outpaces its competitors. While this is perhaps less surprising in comparison to the smaller companies, like Electronic Arts, its success is particularly impressive in comparison to Sony, Microsoft, and Tencent which are not only considerably more sizable than Nintendo but are also considerably more integrated than Nintendo has been. This has been something of concern to some shareholders, resulting in moves by the company to explore ways to integrate its IP and expand its revenue stream.

Integration and Conglomeration

As the company's structure and labor practices make clear, one of the most crucial features of Nintendo is that in spite of its impressive global status, the company has largely avoided integration for most of its history. Instead, it has relied upon licensing and outsourcing for much of its product development. Its primary moves toward integration happened well into the 21st century: opening its own branded stores, opening theme parks based on its IP, and creating its own movie studio.

Nintendo's first notable move into integration was to create retail stores to sell its branded merchandise, in particular Pokémon. The first store was opened in New York City in May 2005 (Wolf, 2005). While the store had been rebranded since, it wasn't until 2019 that it opened a second store in Tokyo, and in 2022, it opened a third in Osaka (Kawasaki, 2022). Similarly, despite decades of having some of the most recognizable characters and the frequent comparisons in the press to Disney, the company's first theme park will be in partnership with Universal Studios Japan and isn't slated to open until early 2023 (Parkin, 2020; Parker, 2022). But the company is moving to open similar parks in other countries including Universal Studios parks in the United States as well as in Singapore (Yeo, 2020).

Finally, as previously noted, after years of licensing its IP for films, Nintendo decided to take more control of films based on its products by purchasing Dynamo Pictures, a Tokyo-based production company that had worked on previous licensed films for the company. The studio will be renamed Nintendo Studios at the close of the deal (Morris, 2022). The addition of Illumination's Chris Meledandri was seen as a move designed to help the company maximize the purchase of the studio ("Illumination Boss . . .," 2021). After the success of the Pokémon franchise films, which with seven films earned more than U.S. $293 million in the United States and Canada, it is not surprising that the company might want to take better charge of media production based on its IP (Box Office Mojo, 2023a, 2023b). This is particularly true in light of the failure of the 1993 film *Super Mario Bros.* (Jankel and Morton, 1993) which is estimated to have earned only about U.S. $48 million worldwide (IMDB, 2023). The move to create its own production studio should likely influence its television production as well, which has similarly benefitted from the company's various franchises.

Conclusion

Former Nintendo president frequently noted that because the company was producing a product that wasn't a necessity, the company had to operate differently. This chapter, which draws on the history of the company from Chapter 2, demonstrates many of the distinct ways in which the company has organized itself and the creation of its products in order to work in just such a situation. Much attention has been given to the way in which particular Nintendo products, such as the Wii console, are innovative. However, as this chapter shows, such particular innovations are part of a much larger trajectory in which the company has used a range of choices about how to approach both product manufacture and business management to create a uniquely competitive global media giant. While the company operates in two related markets – video game software and video game hardware – it approaches each in two very different ways. This allows Nintendo to both run in a lean fashion and maximize money and labor spent. Using affordable, often off-the-shelf, components and outsourcing production has allowed the company to maximize the capabilities of a small number of employees. Developing and licensing IP while maintaining strict controls on the software side has allowed it to form useful arrangements with businesses that should be competition even as those arrangements are most often structured in ways that benefit and enhance Nintendo's positions. Such arrangements have allowed Nintendo, though a relatively small company, to have tremendous sway over the industry as well as impressive cultural success, which is taken up in Chapter 4.

References

Associated Press. (1989, February 2). Nintendo is Sued by Atari. *The New York Times.* https://www.nytimes.com/1989/02/02/business/nintendo-is-sued-by-atari.html

Bae, C. M. (2022, September 11). *Why Multiple Companies Sued Nintendo Over The Wii.* SVG. https://www.svg.com/1003029/why-multiple-companies-sued-nintendo-over-the-wii/

Barnes, J. (2021, December 19). Some of Nintendo's Big Legal Victories Over the Years. *Game Rant.* https://gamerant.com/nintendo-legal-victories-king-kong-blockbuster-youtube-copyright/

Box Office Mojo. (2023a). Franchise: Pokémon. *Box Office Mojo.* https://www.boxofficemojo.com/franchise/fr2907148037/

Box Office Mojo. (2023b). Franchises: US & Canada. *Box Office Mojo.* https://www.boxofficemojo.com/franchise/

Boyer, B. (2008, January 18). NPD: 2007 U.S. Game Industry Growth Up 43% To $17.9 Billion. *Game Developer.* https://www.gamedeveloper.com/pc/npd-2007-u-s-game-industry-growth-up-43-to-17-9-billion

Burton, V. L. III (Ed.). (2023). Best-Selling Video Game Consoles, 2021. In *Market Share Reporter* (33rd ed.). Gale: Gale Directory Library. https://link-gale-com.offcampus.lib.washington.edu/apps/doc/JYJYBP397686064/GDL?u=wash_main&sid=bookmark-GDL&xid=36d28fe8

Burton, V. L. III, & Lazich, R. S. (Eds.). (2021). Leading Public Video Game Firms Worldwide, 2018. In *Market Share Reporter* (31st ed.). Gale: Gale Directory Library. https://link-gale-com.offcampus.lib.washington.edu/apps/doc/AHUHEO660302338/GDL?u=wash_main&sid=bookmark-GDL&xid=d3722262

Carpenter, N. (2021, June 1). Nintendo Awarded $2.1M in Pirated Games Lawsuit. *Polygon.* https://www.polygon.com/22462914/nintendo-lawsuit-2-million-damages-rom-universe-pirated-games

Chan, K. H. (2021, December 14). Here's a Snapshot of Nintendo's Convoluted Legal History. *TheGamer.* https://www.thegamer.com/a-snapshot-of-nintendos-convoluted-legal-history/

Choudhury, S. R. (2016, July 28). How "Pokémon Go" Could Pave the Way for More Profits at Nintendo. *CNBC.* https://www.cnbc.com/2016/07/28/nintendo-news-experts-say-pokémon-go-stakeholders-future-is-bright-in-mobile-gaming-and-intellectual-property.html

Company Complex as Its Games. (1996). *The Nikkei Weekly (Japan).* NexisUni.

Counsell, G. (1992). The Only Game in Town. *The Independent (London).* NexisUni.

Dewinter, J. (2015). *Shigeru Miyamoto: Super Mario Bros., Donkey Kong, the Legend of Zelda.* New York: Bloomsbury Academic.

ESA. (2006). *Game Critics Awards.* http://www.gamecriticsawards.com/2006winners.html

Eshkenazi, A. (2017, June 9). *Securing Supplies is No Game for Nintendo.* Association for Supply Chain Management. https://www.ascm.org/ascm-insights/scm-now-impact/securing-supplies-is-no-game-for-nintendo/

Euromonitor International. (2021). *Video Game Industry Market Share.*

Hall, C. (2017, April 5). Japanese Site Estimates Nintendo Spends $257 to Make One Switch. *Polygon.* https://www.polygon.com/2017/4/5/15195638/nintendo-switch-component-cost-estimate

Harding, R. (2008). Nintendo Makes More Profit Per Employee than Goldman. *FT.com.* Global News Stream. https://www.proquest.com/trade-journals/nintendo-makes-more-profit-per-employee-than/docview/229118840/se-2?accountid=14784

Hollensen, S. (2013). The Blue Ocean that Disappeared – The Case of Nintendo Wii. *Journal of Business Strategy, 34*(5), 25–35. https://doi.org/10.1108/JBS-02-2013-0012

Illumination Boss Chris Meledandri Nominated to Join Nintendo Board of Directors. (2021). *Legal Monitor Worldwide.*

IMDB. (2023, January 9). Super Mario Bros. *IMDB.com.* https://www.imdb.com/title/tt0108255/?ref_=fn_al_tt_2

Interview: Forsaking Performance Race, Nintendo Targets Non-Gamers. (2006). *The Nikkei Weekly (Japan).* NexisUni.

Ishizawa, M. (1992). Nintendo's New Game: Competition; Newcomer Sega's CD-ROM, 16-Bit System Make TV Computer Market a 2-Player Contest. *The Nikkei Weekly (Japan).* NexisUni.

Jankel, A., & Morton, R. (Directors). (1993, May 28). *Super Mario Bros.* [Adventure, Comedy, Family]. Allied Filmmakers, Cinergi Pictures Entertainment, Hollywood Pictures.

Japanese TV Game Makers Take Up Production in U.S. (1982). *The Japan Economic Journal.* NexisUni.

Jones, S. E., & Thiruvathukal, G. K. (2012). *Codename Revolution (Platform Studies).* Cambridge: MIT Press.

Kawasaki, N. (2022, November 10). Nintendo Opens Osaka Store as Mario Drives Merchandise Sales. *Nikkei Asia.* https://asia.nikkei.com/Business/Media-Entertainment/Nintendo-opens-Osaka-store-as-Mario-drives-merchandise-sales

Kerr, A. (2017). *Global Games: Production, Circulation, and Policy in the Networked Era.* London: Taylor & Francis Group.

Kumar, A. (2020). *Monopsony Capitalism: Power and Production in the Twilight of the Sweatshop Age.* Cambridge, UK: Cambridge University Press.

Lam, A. (2019, December 4). Nintendo Switch Life Cycle. *Design Life-Cycle.* http://www.designlife-cycle.com/nintendo-switch

Lewis, L., & Inagaki, K. (2020, January 31). Nintendo Sets Out Plans to Unlock Value from IP Treasure Trove. *Financial Times.* https://www.ft.com/content/04ffe0ec-43fe-11ea-a43a-c4b328d9061c

Long-Time Nintendo President to Step Down at End of Month. (2002). *The Nikkei Weekly (Japan).* NexisUni.

Macrotrends.com. (2022a). *Activision Blizzard: Number of Employees 2010–2022 | ATVI.* https://www.macrotrends.net/stocks/charts/ATVI/activision-blizzard/number-of-employees

Macrotrends.com. (2022b). *Electronic Arts: Number of Employees 2010–2022 | EA.* https://www.macrotrends.net/stocks/charts/EA/electronic-arts/number-of-employees

Macrotrends.com. (2022c). *Microsoft: Number of Employees 2010–2022 | MSFT.* https://www.macrotrends.net/stocks/charts/MSFT/microsoft/number-of-employees

Marketcap.com. (2022a). *Activision Blizzard (ATVI) – Market Capitalization.* https://companiesmarketcap.com/activision-blizzard/marketcap/

Marketcap.com. (2022b). *Electronic Arts (EA) – Market Capitalization.* https://companiesmarketcap.com/electronic-arts/marketcap/

Marketcap.com. (2022c). *Microsoft (MSFT) – Market Capitalization.* https://companiesmarketcap.com/microsoft/marketcap/

Marketcap.com. (2022d). *Nintendo (7974.T) – Market Capitalization.* https://companiesmarketcap.com/nintendo/marketcap/

Marketcap.com. (2022e). *Sony (SONY) – Market Capitalization.* https://companiesmarketcap.com/sony/marketcap/

Marketcap.com. (2022f). *Tencent (TCEHY) – Market Capitalization.* https://companiesmarketcap.com/tencent/revenue/

MarketScreener. (2019). *Morpho, Inc. Acquired 20.8% Stake in PUX Corporation from Panasonic Corporation for ¥80 Million | MarketScreener.* https://www.marketscreener.com/quote/stock/MORPHO-INC-11551545/news/Morpho-Inc-acquired-20-8-stake-in-PUX-Corporation-from-Panasonic-Corporation-for-80-million-34071967/

Mauborgne, R., & Kim, W. C. (2005). *Blue Ocean Strategy: How to Create Uncontested Market Space and Make the Competition Irrelevant.* Boston, MA: Harvard Business School Press.

Maxwell, R., & Miller, T. (2012). *Greening the Media.* Oxford: Oxford University Press.

Miege, B. (1987). The Logics at Work in the New Cultural Industries. *Media, Culture and Society, 9,* 273–289.

Miege, B. (1989a). *The Capitalization of Cultural Production.* New York, NY, Bagnolet, France: International General.

Miege, B. (1989b). The Cultural Commodity. In *The Capitalization of Cultural Production* (pp. 20–37). New York, NY; Bagnolet, France: International General.

Mizuno, Y. (1993). Nintendo Sticks to Its Low-Cost Guns; Despite Analysts' Misgivings, President Pursues Simple Strategy. *The Nikkei Weekly (Japan).* NexisUni.

Mochizuki, T. (2022, February 2). Nintendo Cuts Switch Outlook Again on Supply, Logistics Jam. *Bloomberg.com.* https://www.bloomberg.com/news/articles/2022-02-03/nintendo-cuts-switch-outlook-again-on-supply-logistics-jam

Morris, C. (2022, July 14). *Nintendo Just Bought a Movie Studio – What It Means for the Company.* Fast Company. https://www.fastcompany.com/90769479/nintendo-movie-studio-dynamo-pictures

Newzoo. (2016, March 17). Top 25 Companies 2015 by Game Revenues Up 14%. *Newzoo.* https://newzoo.com/insights/articles/game-revenues-top-25-public-companies-14-2015

Newzoo. (2022). Top Public Video Game Companies | By Revenue. *Newzoo.* https://newzoo.com/insights/rankings/top-25-companies-game-revenues

Nichols, R. (2013). Who Plays, Who Pays? Mapping Video Game Production and Consumption Globally. In N. B. Huntemann & B. Aslinger (Eds.), *Gaming Globally: Production, Play and Place* (pp. 19–39). New York: Palgrave MacMillan.

Nichols, R. (2014). *The Video Game Business (International Screen Industries).* New York, NY: Palgrave Macmillan on Behalf of the British Film Institute.

Nichols, R. (2020). Pokémon Go: Globalization. In M. T. Payne & N. B. Huntemann (Eds.), *How to Play Video Games* (pp. 250–258). New York, USA: New York University Press. https://doi.org/10.18574/9781479830404-032

Nintendo. (2003). *Annual Report, 2002.* https://www.nintendo.co.jp/ir/pdf/2002/annual0203e.pdf

Nintendo. (2004). *Annual Report, 2003.* https://www.nintendo.co.jp/ir/pdf/2003/annual0303e.pdf

Nintendo. (2005). *Annual Report, 2004.* Nintendo, Ltd.

Nintendo. (2006). *Annual Report, 2005.* https://www.nintendo.co.jp/ir/pdf/2005/annual0503e.pdf

Nintendo. (2007). *Annual Report, 2006.* Nintendo, Ltd.

Nintendo. (2008). *Annual Report, 2007.* Nintendo, Ltd.

Nintendo. (2009). *Annual Report, 2009.* Nintendo, Ltd.

Nintendo. (2010). *Annual Report, 2010.* Nintendo, Ltd.

Nintendo. (2011). *Annual Report, 2011.* Nintendo, Ltd.

Nintendo. (2012). *Annual Report, 2012.* https://www.nintendo.co.jp/ir/pdf/2012/annual1203e.pdfww.nintendo.co.jp/ir/pdf/2013/annual1303e.pdf

Nintendo. (2013). *Annual Report, 2013.* https://www.nintendo.co.jp/ir/pdf/2013/annual1303e.pdf

Nintendo. (2014). *Annual Report, 2014.* https://www.nintendo.co.jp/ir/pdf/2014/annual1403e.pdf

Nintendo. (2015). *Annual Report, 2015.* Nintendo, Ltd.

Nintendo. (2016). *Annual Report, 2016.* Nintendo, Ltd.

Nintendo. (2017). *Annual Report, 2017.* Nintendo, Ltd.

Nintendo. (2018). *Annual Report, 2018.* Nintendo, Ltd.

Nintendo. (2019). *Annual Report, 2019.* Nintendo, Ltd.

Nintendo. (2020). *Annual Report, 2020.* Nintendo, Ltd.

Nintendo. (2021). *Annual Report, 2021.* Nintendo, Ltd.

Nintendo. (2022a). *Annual Report, 2022.* Nintendo, Ltd.

Nintendo. (2022b). *Corporate Information: Directors/Executive Officers.* Nintendo, Ltd. http://www.nintendo.co.jp/corporate/en/officer/index.html

Nintendo. (2022c). *Corporate Information: Principal Offices and Facilities.* Nintendo, Ltd. https://www.nintendo.co.jp/corporate/en/offices/index.html

Nintendo. (2022d, December 23). *CSR Information.* Nintendo, Ltd. https://www.nintendo.co.jp/csr/en/index.html

Nintendo Continues Streak of Super Profits, Mulls Next Move. (2008). *The Nikkei Weekly (Japan).* NexisUni.

Nintendo Observer. (2022). *NCL:* "Notice Regarding Changes of Representative Director and Other Management" (Nintendo FY3/2018). *Nintendo Observer.* https://nintendobserver.com/2018/05/ncl-notice-regarding-changes-of-representative-director-and-other-management-nintendo-fy3-2018/

Nishimura.com. (2022). *Professionals: Asa Shinkawa | Nishimura & Asahi.* https://www.nishimura.com/en/attorney/0024.html

Parker, R. (2022, December 14). Universal Studios Hollywood Announces Opening Date for Super Nintendo World. *People.com.* https://people.com/travel/super-nintendo-world-universal-studios-hollywood-opening-date/

Parkin, S. (2020, December 20). Shigeru Miyamoto Wants to Create a Kinder World. *The New Yorker.* https://www.newyorker.com/culture/the-new-yorker-interview/shigeru-miyamoto-wants-to-create-a-kinder-world

Quast, J., Najarro, J., & Deo, S. (2021, October 16). 1 Way That Nintendo is Finally Leveraging Its Valuable Intellectual Property. *The Motley Fool.* https://www.nasdaq.com/articles/1-way-that-nintendo-is-finally-leveraging-its-valuable-intellectual-property-2021-10-16

Rad, C., & Otero, J. (2017, May 1). Nintendo Reveals Restructuring Plans. *IGN.* https://www.ign.com/articles/2015/09/14/nintendo-reveals-restructuring-plans

Ruggill, J., McAllister, K., Nichols, R., & Kaufman, R. (2016). *Inside the Video Game Industry: Game Developers Talk about the Business of Play*. London: Taylor & Francis Group.

Ryan, J. (2011). *Super Mario: How Nintendo Conquered America*. New York: Portfolio Penguin.

Saijo, K. (2007). Nintendo's Non-Japanese Approach. *The Nikkei Weekly (Japan)*. NexisUni.

Shay, R., & Palomba, A. (2020). First-Party Success or First-Party Failure? A Case Study on Audience Perceptions of the Nintendo Brand During the Wii U's Product Life Cycle. *Games and Culture*, *15*(5), 475–500.

Shen, X. (2020, February 19). Here's Where Your Favorite Gadgets are Made, from the Nintendo Switch to Apple AirPods Pro. *South China Morning Post*. https://www.scmp.com/abacus/tech/article/3051433/heres-where-your-favorite-gadgets-are-made-nintendo-switch-apple

Sirani, J. (2021, February 17). All the Lawsuits Nintendo is Facing Over Joy-Con Drift. *IGN*. https://www.ign.com/articles/all-the-lawsuits-nintendo-is-facing-over-joy-con-drift

Sloan, D. (2011). *Playing to Wiin: Nintendo and the Video Game Industry's Greatest Comeback*. Singapore: Wiley Asia.

Statista. (2022a). *Sony Group Number of Employees 2022*. Statista. https://www.statista.com/statistics/638777/sony-group-number-of-employees/

Statista. (2022b). *Tencent: Number of Employees 2021*. Statista. https://www.statista.com/statistics/223719/number-of-tencent-group-employees/

Stelter, B. (2010). Xbox Console Makers Focus on Other Media and Uses. *The Ledger*. http://proquest.umi.com/pqdweb?did=2077530031&Fmt=7&clientId=5258&RQT=309&VName=PQD

Tang, M. (2019). *Tencent: The Political Economy of China's Surging Internet Giant*. Taylor & Francis Group. https://doi.org/10.4324/9780429202896

Tedder, M. (2022, July 14). Nintendo Makes a Move to Take on Disney, Universal. *TheStreet*. https://www.thestreet.com/investing/nintendo-makes-a-move-to-take-on-disney-universal

Tedesco, T. (2009). iPhone Economy Taking Shape; Apps World. *National Post*, FP.1.

Tomaselli, F., Luiz, T., Di Serio, L., Luciel, S., & de Oliveira, L. (2008, May 9). *Value Chain Management and Competitive Strategy in the Home Video Game Industry*. POMS 19th Annual Conference, La Jolla, CA. file:///Users/rjnic/Downloads/Value_Chain_Management_and_Competitive_Strategy_in.pdf

TradingEconomics.com. (2022). *Tencent Holdings | 700– Employees Total Number*. https://tradingeconomics.com/700:hk:employees

Unozawa, S. (2002). Nintendo Sees Generational Change. *The Nikkei Weekly (Japan)*. NexisUni.

VGChartz.com. (2022a). Global Yearly Video Game Chart, 2013. *VGChartz*. https://www.vgchartz.com

VGChartz.com. (2022b). Global Yearly Video Game Chart, 2014. *VGChartz*. https://www.vgchartz.com

VGChartz.com. (2022c). Global Yearly Video Game Chart, 2015. *VGChartz*. https://www.vgchartz.com

VGChartz.com. (2022d). Global Yearly Video Game Chart, 2016. *VGChartz*. https://www.vgchartz.com

VGChartz.com. (2022e). Global Yearly Video Game Chart, 2017. *VGChartz.* https://www.vgchartz.com

VGChartz.com. (2022f). Platform Totals. *VGChartz.* https://www.vgchartz.com

VGChartz.com. (2022g). *Total Worldwide Platform Totals.* https://www.vgchartz.com/analysis/platform_totals

Wales, M. (2006, May 15). Red Steel UK Review. *IGN.* https://www.ign.com/articles/2006/11/24/red-steel-uk-review

Weber, L. (2017, April 11). Outside Workers Fuel Videogame Industry. *Wall Street Journal.* Global News Stream. https://www.proquest.com/newspapers/outside-workers-fuel-videogame-industry-house/docview/1886169796/se-2?accountid=14784

Wesley, D. T. A., & Barczak, G. (2010). *Innovation and Marketing in the Video Game Industry: Avoiding the Performance Trap.* Farnham, Surrey, England: Gower.

Whitehead, T. (2013, September 27). Nintendo Acquires 27% of Panasonic's PUX Technology, Which Includes Voice Recognition. *Nintendo Life.* https://www.nintendolife.com/news/2013/09/nintendo_acquires_27_percent_of_panasonicrs_pux_technology_which_includes_voice_recognition

Wijman, T. (2020a, May 8). The World's 2.7 Billion Gamers Will Spend $159.3 Billion on Games in 2020; The Market Will Surpass $200 Billion by 2023. *Newzoo.* https://newzoo.com/insights/articles/newzoo-games-market-numbers-revenues-and-audience-2020-2023/

Wijman, T. (2020b, November 4). Global Game Revenues Up an Extra $15 Billion This Year as Engagement Skyrockets. *Newzoo.* https://newzoo.com/insights/articles/game-engagement-during-covid-pandemic-adds-15-billion-to-global-games-market-revenue-forecast/

Witkowski, W. (2021, January 2). Videogames are a Bigger Industry than Movies and North American Sports Combined, Thanks to the Pandemic. *MarketWatch.* https://www.marketwatch.com/story/videogames-are-a-bigger-industry-than-sports-and-movies-combined-thanks-to-the-pandemic-11608654990

Wolf, A. (2005). Nintendo Opening 1st "World" Store. *TWICE, 20*(10), 104.

Wong, J. (2022, February 4). For Sony and Nintendo, the Supply-Chain Pile-Up Is Just a Speed Bump. *Wall Street Journal.* https://www.wsj.com/articles/for-sony-and-nintendo-the-supply-chain-pile-up-is-just-a-speed-bump-11643972945

WSJ. (2022). NTDOY Company Profile & Executives – Nintendo Co. Ltd. ADR. *Wall Street Journal.* https://www.wsj.com/market-data/quotes/NTDOY/company-people/executive-profile/147206474

Yeo, J. (2020, December 19). Super Mario Creator Confirms Plans for Super Nintendo World to Open in S'pore. *Mothership.sg.* https://mothership.sg/2020/12/super-nintendo-world-singapore-uss/

Zippia.com. (2022, March 25). Activision Blizzard Number of Employees, Statistics, Diversity, Demographics, and Facts. *Zippia.* https://www.zippia.com/activision-blizzard-careers-155/demographics/

4 Nintendo's Cultural and Political Profile

When the Summer 2020 Olympic Games opened in Tokyo, Japan, the ceremony included music and references from a number of Japanese video games, including *Final Fantasy*, *Kingdom Hearts*, and *Monster Hunter*. Glaringly absent was Japan's most famous video game export, the Nintendo character Mario. What is perhaps more surprising is that a number of Nintendo franchises, including Mario, were originally intended to be part of the ceremony, with at least one version of the plans including popular music star Lady Gaga performing in an outfit that would pay homage to Nintendo property Mario and exiting the stage via a pipe similar to those used in the Mario games. Ultimately, however, Nintendo withdrew from the ceremony (Skrebels, 2021). While the invitation to participate in such a prestigious global event surely speaks to Nintendo's prestige, the decision to pull out gives just as clear an example of how powerful and insulated the company is. While it is unclear exactly why the company withdrew from the ceremony, one likely reason has to do with how closely the company has guarded its intellectual property (IP) over the years. This chapter looks at the way Nintendo's various products and strategies have contributed to its cultural and political profile. It draws on the history established in Chapter 2 and the economic profile in Chapter 3 to better understand how Nintendo has worked to foster its profile around the world.

Nintendo, Intellectual Property, and Brand Management

Nintendo's management of its IP has been frequently a point of contention for outside observers. As Payne (2019) notes, fans have often expressed frustration over the company's redeployment of a few select franchises, while investors were frustrated about the company's slow moves to make use of that IP to enter the lucrative mobile arena (Kumar, 2014). This approach can best be understood as the company wanting to simultaneously emphasize its importance in the longer history of the games industry while also curating brand perception and minimize risk to that perception. But it also serves to emphasize certain

DOI: 10.4324/9781003031918-4

types of game play as well as characters and locations (both in game and out-side) that are central to the company's long-term view of itself. And, of course, this serves to engender nostalgia to the game's long-term audiences even as it helps to educate new players just entering the fold (Payne, 2019).

Such tight controls aren't surprising. As discussed in Chapter 2, with Nin-tendo's success buoying the games industry from its emergence through the rise of Sony and Microsoft, for an entire generation of game players, Nintendo became virtually synonymous with video games. In that period, many of their most popular pieces of IP were initially established, and some of them became particularly notable. It was noted that in 1990, Mario was more recognized in the United States than Micky Mouse (Coates, 1993; Sheff, 1993).

Table 4.1 shows the best-selling franchises owned by Nintendo as of 2021. One clear pattern is just how many of the company's franchises began prior to the year 2000. But it's also worth noting how many of them are tied to the company's biggest platform successes. Three of these – *Duck Hunt*, the

Table 4.1 Best-Selling Nintendo Franchises, by Units Sold, 2021

Franchise	First Game and Year of Release	Initial Platform	Total Franchise Units Sold
Luigi	*Luigi's Mansion* (2001)	GameCube	20,000,000
Wario	*Super Mario Land 2: 6 Golden Coins* (1992)	Game Boy	22,000,000
Yoshi	*Super Mario World* (1990)	Super Famicom/ Super NES	28,100,000
Duck Hunt	*Duck Hunt* (1984)	Famiicom/NES	28,310,000
Nintendogs	*Nintendogs* (2005)	DS	28,600,000
Brain Age	*Brain Age: train Your Brain in Minutes a Day* (2005)	DS	33,000,000
Kirby	*Kirby's Dream Land* (1992)	Game Boy	38,000,000
Game & Watch	*Ball* (1980)	Game & Watch	43,000,000
Donkey Kong	*Donkey Kong* (1981)	Arcade	58,000,000
Animal Crossing	*Animal Crossing* (2001)	N64	59,000,000
Super Smash Bros.	*Super Smash Bros.* (1999)	N64	62,000,000
The Legend of Zelda	*The Legend of Zelda* (1986)	Famicom/NES	103,000,000
Wii	*Wii Sports* (2006)	Wii	202,000,000
Pokémon	*Pocket Monsters: Red and Green* (1996)	Game Boy	495,000,000
Mario	*Donkey Kong* (1981)	Arcade	653,000,000

Source: (Jurkovich, 2021; Martin, 2021)

Game & Watch series, and the Wii series of games – owe their success to their inclusion with the console itself at the time of sale. The Game & Watch, which initially was an integrated piece of hardware and software unable to play any other games, ultimately became a franchise of its own with the ability to expand (Jurkovich, 2021). In spite of that success, as noted in Chapter 3, Nintendo has been relatively hesitant to leverage its IP outside of games. In part, this may owe to some early failures, such as the 1993 film *Super Mario Bros.*, which was a box-office flop (Stuart, 2018). But the success of the Pokémon franchise, however, would seem to offer a powerful counter-example. The franchise spawned not just numerous games, but trading cards, multiple films, a globally popular television show in addition to a wide range of merchandise (Nichols, 2020). Payne (2019) attributes this to a desire to curate the company's legacy and expectations of its players. He calls this practice "world reinforcing" in contrast to franchise management which is about worldbuilding and world sharing as defined by Jenkins (2006) and Johnson (2013), respectively. This careful, curatorial management of legacy is a clear pattern in Nintendo's practices, which helps to make sense of how long it took a company so frequently compared to Disney to begin to explore integration. It requires us to factor Nintendo's attention to its brand into any understanding of the company and its decisions as a factor as important as its approach to product development, revenue management, or employee relations.

Nintendo IP in Other Media

With this in mind, Nintendo's approach to the licensing of its IP has been both careful in its approach and attentive to curating not just for a long-term audience, but to also expanding the range of media forms that audiences might be able to use to interact with their IP. Throughout much of the company's history, this has involved partnering with trusted companies in other areas, though as noted in previous chapters, Nintendo has begun to diversity for better control. Most of these partnerships have been in visual media – film and television – and, to a lesser extent, publishing.

Film and Television

Of particular interest are the company's moves to explore film and television. As Table 4.2 shows, the company has attempted to develop a range of films and feature-length anime based on its IP, though they have not always been as successful as the company might have hoped.[1] As the previous chapter noted, the company did eventually expand toward developing its own animation rather than always seeking outside partnerships.

What is perhaps most noteworthy in examining the company's approach to film is the way in which the type of film has changed in terms of both format

Table 4.2 Films and Feature-Length Anime Based on Nintendo Intellectual Property

Film Title and Year of Release	Global or Country of Release	Initial Format	Total Box Office or Sales (Millions of U.S. Dollars)
Super Mario Bros.: The Great Mission to Rescue Princess Peach (1986)	Japan	VHS	Unknown
The Wizard (1989)	Global	Feature film	$14.3
Super Mario Bros. (1993)	Global	Feature Film	$20.9
Mario Kirby Meisaku (1995)	Japan	Educational VHS	Unknown
Pokémon: The First Movie – Mewtwo Strikes Back (1998)	Global	Feature Film	$163.6
Pokémon the Movie 2000 (1999)	Global	Feature film	$133.9
Pokémon 3 the Movie: Spell of the Unknown (2000)	Global	Feature film	$68.4
Pokémon 4Ever: Celebi – Voice of the Forest (2001)	Global	Feature film	$28
Pokémon Heroes (2002)	Global	Feature film	$20.9
Animal Crossing: The Movie (2006)	Japan	Feature Film	$16.2
Pokémon: Detective Pikachu (2019)	Global	Feature Film	$449.8

Source: (Box Office Mojo; 2023; "*Gekijô-ban . . .*," 2023; "*Gekijô-ban poketto . . .*," 2023; Kurland, 2021; "List of. . .," 2023; Rakuten.com, 2012; "*Sûpâ Mario . . .*,"2023)

and release. Most of the company's first forays into film were targeted primarily at the Japanese market, until roughly 1990s when video games began to become more mainstream. The example of the 1989 film *The Wizard* marks a moment where both the games and the company began to achieve truly mainstream, global success. While the film was not exclusively about Nintendo IP, Nintendo IP was central to the film, with Super Mario Bros. serving as the key piece of software in the film's climax (Holland, 1989). Following this, the company began more focused uses of its IP in film, first focusing on characters related to Mario, and then achieving the most success with a number of films based on Pokémon. Worth noting is that the company has not limited itself to animated films and has increasingly begun to experiment with ways to use their particularly popular pieces of IP in novel ways, such as the 2019 film Detective Pikachu, which moves from the more literal "gotta catch 'em all"[2] plot as a way to introduce new Pokémon that was prevalent in the previous films to an original story making use of the characters in a distinctly novel way (Letterman, 2019).

The company's approach to television has followed a similar pattern. Table 4.3 provides a breakdown of television shows based on Nintendo properties. As it makes clear, the company has long engaged in using television

Table 4.3 Television Series and Anime Based on Nintendo Properties

Show Title	Country of Origin	Production Company	Years Ran
Saturday Supercade	United States	Ruby-Spears Productions, Taft Entertainment Television	1983–1985
Amada Anime Series: Super Mario Bros.	Japan	Studio Juno	1989
The Super Mario Bros. Super Show!	United States, Canada	DiC Entertainment, Dakota Pictures	1989
The Legend of Zelda	United States, Canada	DiC Entertainment, Dakota Pictures	1989
Captain N: The Game Master	United States, Canada	DiC Entertainment, Saban Productions	1989–1991
King Koopa's Kool Kartoons	United States	DiC Entertainment	1989–1990
The Adventures of Super Mario Bros. 3	United States	DiC Entertainment	1990
The Super Mario Challenge	United Kingdom	The Children's Channel	1990–1991
Super Mario World	United States, Canada	DiC Entertainment, Retitalia	1991
Captain N & the Video Game Masters	United States, Canada	DiC Entertainment	1992–1993
Super Mario All Stars	Japan, United States	DiC Entertainment	1994
Fire Emblem	Japan	Intelligent Systems, KSS	1995
Donkey Kong Country	France, Canada	Canal+, France 2, Hong Guang Animation	1996–2000
Donkey Kong Planet	France	Media Lab	1996–2000
Kirby: Right Back at Ya!	Japan	Warpstar, HAL Laboratory	2002–2006
F-Zero GP Legend	Japan	DENTSU Music and Entertainment	2003–2005
Pokémon	Japan	Creatures, GAME FREAK	1997–2023
Pokémon Journeys: The Series	Japan	OLM Incorporated	2019–

Source: ("Amada . . .," 2023; "Captain N: The Game . . .," 2023; Donkey Kong Country, 2023; "F-Zero . . .," 2023; *Faia emuburemu*, 2023; "King Koopa's . . .," 2023; "Kirby . . .," 2023; Knight, 2022; "List of . . .," 2023; Pokémon, 2023; "Pokémon Journeys . . .," 2023; "Pokémon Master . . .," 2023; "Saturday . . .," 2023; Super Mario All-Stars, 2023; Super Mario World, 2023; "The Adventures of . . .," 2023; "The Super Mario Bros. Super . . .," 2023; The Super Mario Challenge, 2023)

shows, particularly cartoons, as a way to encourage engagement with many of its key franchises. In many cases, a particular series was timed to release at the same time as the game it was linked to ("List of . . .," 2023). Further, as the previous chapter noted, Nintendo has been cautious in choosing which companies it partnered with to license its IP. In the case of most of its early cartoons, the company worked with DiC Entertainment, a company that not only worked on cartoon adaptations for other game companies including Capcom and Sega, but that also had an extensive history with children's animation and cross-cultural translation of properties. DiC began in France and later partnered with Japanese company Tokyo Movie Shinsha, before expanding into the U.S. market in the early 1980s (Perlmutter, 2014; "Ulysse 31," 2023). Because of the importance the U.S. and European markets would take in the coming decades, finding an animation partner that could help the company adapt its products across markets was vital.

But Nintendo also approached markets differently, releasing television shows and games in different orders depending upon whether the market was established or being cultivated. The best example of this can be seen with the company's approach to its Pokémon products, which include not just video games but also television shows, feature films, and tremendously popular trading cards (Nichols, 2014). In Japan, both the Pokémon video game and cards were released at the same time; in other markets, such as the United States, the company began by releasing the television show and the video games first, followed by the associated cards (Nichols, 2020; "Fabulous History . . .," 1999). Further, as particular media markets have changed, Nintendo has changed its approach to using them as well. While most of the television shows listed were released in partnership with national partners for syndication, with *Pokémon Journeys*, the company instead opted to release to streaming platform Netflix in the United States (Porter, 2020). Finally, it is clear the company has been willing to experiment with different formats, not only in terms of the program type but also within the program itself. While most of the entries are animation, the U.K. program *Super Mario Challenge* was a game show. In addition, a number of the programs themselves incorporated live action elements, typically with actors playing key Nintendo characters in sketches between cartoons. The most notable of these was the portrayal of Mario by former wrestler Captain Lou Albano in *The Super Mario Bros. Super Show* ("List of . . .," 2023).

Publishing

In contrast, Nintendo's approach to publishing has been more varied in its approach. The company's portfolio of intellectual properties makes it ideal for a range of approaches, in part because the company has done so well targeting youth with some of its products while engendering deep fan connection. This has resulted in the company being well represented both in book publishing and in magazines. In the area of book publishing, the company has partnered with a number of notable publishers, including Random House, Simon & Schuster, and Darkhorse publishing (Patterson, 2018; Simon and Schuster, 2023; Dark Horse, 2023). The books published range from stories based on popular characters and series to detailed encyclopedias of particular game worlds and other products targeted at the fandoms of specific IP.

72 Nintendo's Cultural and Political Profile

Because of the sizable fandoms of Nintendo products, cultivated over multiple decades, there has been an extensive history of magazines published in a variety of countries devoted to Nintendo and its various products. Table 4.4 provides a breakdown of these magazines. It is likely that there are others, as it is almost certain there are a number of small, unofficial publications and zines dedicated to Nintendo properties. Indeed, Nintendo itself ran a number of official enterprises geared toward cultivating fandom including the long-running Club Nintendo, a customer loyalty program, and its successor My Nintendo. Club Nintendo ran from 2003 until 2015, and was discontinued at the crucial moment (Chowdhry, 2015; Nintendo, 2015). Those loyalty programs got surprisingly late starts, given the first magazines focused on Nintendo began publishing more than a decade earlier.

But as Table 4.4 clearly shows, Nintendo's popularity has justified magazines in a number of countries. As discussed in previous chapters, Nintendo has

Table 4.4 Magazines Devoted to Nintendo Coverage

Magazine Title	Country of Origin	Years Running	Publisher
Dengeki Nintendo	Japan	1992–	ASCII Media Works
Mean Machines	United Kingdom	1990–1992	EMAP
NF Magazine/ Nintendo Force	United States	2013	NF Publishing, LLC
NGC Magazine	Great Britain	1997–2006	Future PLC
Nintendo Fun Club	United States	1987–1988	Nintendo
Nintendo Gamer	United Kingdom	2006–2012	Future PLC
Nintendo La Rivista Ufficiale	Italy	2002–2013	Sprea Media Italy/ Future
Nintendo Magazine System	Australia	1993–2000	Catalyst Publishing
Nintendo Power	United States	1998–2013	Nintendo/Future US
Nintendo World	Brazil	1998	Conrad Editora
Nintendomagasinet	Sweden	1990–1994	Atlantic Förlag
Official Nintendo Magazine	Great Britain	2006–2014	Future PLC
Pure Nintendo Magazine	United States	2011–	Pure Media, LLC
Revista Oficial Nintendo	Spain	1992–2018	HobbyPress
Super Play	Great Britain	1992–1996	Future PLC
Super Play	Sweden	1993–2009	Hjemmet Mortensen
Switch Player	United Kingdom	2017–	Paul Murphy/Issuu
Total!	United Kingdom	1991–1996	Future PLC

Source: ("A Brief History . . .," 2019; AusiReprints, 2023; Beer, 2008; Cifaldi, 2012; Dengeki, 2023; Figueroa, 2018; Future International Licensing, 2008; Gaines, 2016; GamesRadar, 2012; Gonzalez, 2012; Herranz, 2018; Hrin, 2017; Intervista, n.d.; Issuu, n.d.; McFerran, 2011; MCV, 2012; "Nintendo and Future . . .," 2013; Nintendomagasinet, 1990; Nintendo Rivista . . ., n.d.; Official Nintendo . . ., 2013; ONM, 2014; Plunkett, 2012; Rougeau, n.d.; Scullion, 2012; Steve Jarratt Interview, n.d.; Wikipedia, 2022, 2023a, 2023b)

grown to value markets outside of Japan in waves, with the North American market coming to prominence first, followed by various European countries. But the continued presence of British publishing giant Future PLC is notable not only because of the number of magazines they have published focused on Nintendo over the years but also because the company has been platform agnostic. The company also published magazines related to the Microsoft Xbox and Sony PlayStation consoles as well as older computer platforms like the Commodore 64 and Amiga. Its more recent industry history includes publications like *GamesRadar* and *Edge* (Future PLC, 2023; Future Publishing, 2023).

Nintendo's Political Profile

The success of Nintendo IP across a range of media ultimately results in the company's ability to exercise considerable political and cultural power well beyond the borders of Japan. It would be simple to assume that this has primarily resulted in conflict between the company and various countries and their governments, the reality is much more complex. Nor would it be correct to assume that Nintendo exerts that power in either clumsy or overt ways. As an example of those complexities, a number of countries became concerned over how the game *Pokémon Go* would encroach on sensitive cultural or political spaces. The game, which asked players using their smart phones to check-in at real places, in order to capture Pokémon, battle other players, and receive prizes based on where they visited. The locations for these encounters, referred to in-game as PokéStops, initially included a range of places including retailers, churches, and other spots of local interest also included such spaces as the Holocaust Museum in Washington, D.C., the Holy Kaaba and Grand Mosque in Mecca, and the Auschwitz Museum in Germany. Moreover, a number of these sites were government buildings and battle sites. This resulted in a number of governments including those of Russia, Kuwait, and Egypt seeking bans on playing the game near government sites (Akhtar, 2016; "Nations of the World . . .," 2016; Nichols, 2020; "Pokémon Mania . . .," 2016). Perhaps most significantly, Saudi Arabian clerics introduced a fatwa banning the game as a form of gambling (Stanglin, 2016).

But by 2023, Saudi Arabia became the biggest investor in the Nintendo, with the country's Public Investment Fund owning more than 8 percent of the company's shares (Mochizuki and Furukawa, 2023). That was not the first example of government investment in the company. In 2002, the Japanese government purchased a 1.4 percent stake in the company, though its rationale was different: to forestall too many shares from being released. By 2007, at the request of Nintendo, those shares were sold off, to help the company's liquidity (Jenkins, 2007). Both cases serve as examples not only of the significance of the company, but also of its potential to exercise soft power in a range of markets and countries. Likewise, the company's own policies are one of its most significant means of exercising political and cultural power. In 2021, the company formally recognized the rights of same-sex couples to enjoy shared benefits, in spite of the Japanese government's refusal to do so. The move was seen as particularly significant because Japanese courts had recently upheld a ban on same-sex marriages. As such, the company's move marks an important moment of overt political leadership. However, much of the company's lobbying happens through industrial associations. Tracing membership in these associations is challenging; however, among the groups the company is known to belong to are the North American trade groups the Entertainment Software Association and the Entertainment Software Association of Canada as well as the Interactive Software Federation of Europe (ESAC, 2019; ISFE, 2023; Santucci, 2023).

Nintendo and Litigation

From the earliest days of the video game industry, litigation has served as one of the chief mechanisms for exercising power. In less than a year of Atari's *Pong* was released, it was already the subject of what might well be the first lawsuit in the industry, one centered on patent concerns (Ford, 2012). Since that time, litigation has only grown in importance as a tool for game companies to exercise their political power. Nintendo is no different in this regard. Indeed, perhaps the clearest example of Nintendo's political power is less overt, happening through a range of legal system as a mechanism to protect the company's IP and other interests. Rather than attempting to compile a complete list of the litigation Nintendo has been involved in across the range of countries its various products are produced from and sold in, what follows is a brief discussion of key areas of litigation the company has been involved in with a list of particularly noteworthy cases. As discussed in Chapter 2, almost from the time the company entered into the global games market, it has been involved in a range of court cases in its various markets, touching on a wide variety of issues including IP, antitrust, unfair trade practices, and consumer related issues. The occurrence of these suits has tended to follow the company's own trends: as new markets became more or less important, the likelihood of litigation changed in response. When new pieces of hardware were brought to market, the type of IP cases likewise shifted. As in any litigation, claimants typically tried to bring their suits in the jurisdictions where the laws seemed most favorable. Finally, some of these cases were brought by Nintendo, helping to establish its reputation in the industry as particularly litigious, while others were brought by competitors, members of the company's supply chain, consumers, and, more recently, private businesses and individuals unaffiliated with the company (Chan, 2021; Mitchell, 2016).

Antitrust

One of the first major suits Nintendo was involved in focused on antitrust concerns. In February 1989, the Atari Corporation initiated a lawsuit against Nintendo, citing the restrictions Nintendo required for licensing as a developer with the company (AP, 1989). Those licensing restrictions, discussed briefly in Chapter 2, were focused on protecting the company against cheap knock-off games which had been a major contributor the games industry in the 1980s and, particularly, to the major console manufacturers including Atari (Nichols, 2014). Nintendo's licensing rules stopped developers from publishing games developed for Nintendo on competing consoles. This was problematic, in part, because Nintendo games were using special chips to allow them to play, but there was a shortage of those chips (AP, 1989; Lunney, 1989). Nintendo ultimately won the suit, but a similar complaint was filed in 1991 by American Video Entertainment, again focused on the microchips required for a game to work on Nintendo consoles (MacLean, 1991; Weber, 1992). As discussed previously, these suits ultimately had little impact, as Nintendo's licensing deals with developers ultimately became a primary model for the rest of the industry. This would not be the company's last antitrust complaint, and it would not always be as successful. In 2002, the European Union (EU) fined the company and seven of its distributors over antitrust violations (Shishkin, 2002). It was ruled that Nintendo and its distributors had colluded in order to keep prices of Nintendo products artificially high in the EU from 1991 to 1996 ("Commission Fines . . .," 2002). The fines impacted distributors in the United Kingdom, Ireland, Italy, Portugal, Sweden, Denmark, Finland, Iceland, Belgium, Luxembourg, and Greece, though a majority of the fine was levied against Nintendo itself (Van Hassteren and Peña Castellot, 2002). While the impact of these suits did little to slow Nintendo's dominance within the industry, they have served as touchstones for more recent antitrust suits against other companies within the industry, particularly Microsoft, which cited the various Nintendo antitrust rulings as a defense in a lawsuit of its own, and in 2022 when it announced its intention to acquire rival game company Activision Blizzard (Razak, 2010; Kharpal, 2022).

Copyright and Piracy

Not surprisingly, most of the cases Nintendo has brought against others have centered around protecting its IP. As noted in Chapters 2 and 3, one key area has centered around anti-piracy measures, and China, in particular, has been a repeated area of focus for the company ("100 Million . . .," 1995; Gaudiosi, 2005; Nakanishi, 2003; "Nintendo to Make . . .," 1993). The company takes the issue seriously enough that in 2014, it hired a lobbying firm in the United States specifically to address piracy concerns (Olney, 2014). But Nintendo's attempts at using IP law have extended beyond piracy to a range of other areas.

One of the earliest examples of Nintendo's use of IP law was its 1989 lawsuit in the United States against video rental chain Blockbuster. Seeking to limit loss of revenue to game rentals, the company sued, noting that Blockbuster had been including copies of game instruction manuals as the center of the suit (Forman, 1989). Ultimately, the courts ruled in favor of Blockbuster, though the rental chain was also required to use third-party manuals with its game rentals (Chan, 2021). But the suit was telling in how Nintendo would approach the protection of its copyright. Because video game content relies so heavily on interaction, and because Nintendo has been so successful in building up both loyalty and nostalgia for its products, one of the biggest challenges the company faces is the desire of fans and content creators to make use of its IP. Again using favorable U.S. copyright protections, particularly the Digital Millennium Copyright Act (DMCA), the company has worked to have removed fan-made games, YouTube videos and trailers, and even game tournaments stopped or removed from their respective platforms (Chan, 2021). But similar suits have been issued elsewhere. In 2017, the company sued MariCar, a business in Japan which was renting go-karts and Nintendo-themed costumes to consumers to drive around a range of locations. Courts ruled in Nintendo's favor, using a Japanese law known in English as the Unfair Competition Prevention Act (UCPA), noting that the use of a company name known among gamers as a reference to the Nintendo game *Mario Kart* series of games, as well as costumes based on the likeness of characters from game was an infringement (Shimada, 2019).

One area this has particular impact is in the area of fan "modding." While there are different ways of defining modding, a useful way to think about it comes from Wallace (2014) who defines modding as "the process of altering, adding to, or deleting [software] code to change the way that [the software] works." As Lee (2022) notes, modding is a practice that U.S. IP law struggles to address adequately, even as emerging technologies and game complexity make it increasingly common. Perhaps the most salient challenge for game companies is that anyone likely to create a mod is almost certainly only going to do so because of a deep connection to content itself. For companies like Nintendo this poses a problem, because creating that level of connection has been vital to the company's success, and so such suits risk alienating some of their best customers. In 2016, the company issued takedown orders for over 500 games alone, some of which had taken years of time for fans to develop (Buckley, 2016; Orland, 2016).

The company has also gone after a number of ROM sites. ROM sites contain complete software programs copied from ROM chips. These are typically emulations of software from previous consoles that is no longer available (Chan, 2021; Carpenter, 2021). Such sites may contain hundreds of games, which, given the company's popularity and work in cultivating its fandoms, isn't so surprising. But the company has been aggressive numerous sites, seeking multimillion dollar awards (Chan, 2021). These suits have typically been filed in the United States and United Kingdom and have resulted in both civil and criminal charges (Carpenter, 2021). In one criminal suit, Gary Bowser, who created and shared devices designed to circumvent the Nintendo Switch's protections, was sentenced to three years in a U.S. prison and to a $10 million fine (Good, 2023).

A second are of conflict stems from the nature of in-game purchases. The games industry, including Nintendo, has increasingly moved to create new revenue streams beyond individual sales and subscriptions to online games. In-game purchases have become a lucrative revenue stream, particularly in the mobile and casual games markets, but in other games as well. As Rossow (2016) notes, games like Nintendo's mobile game created with Niantic *Pokémon Go* include a number of in-game purchases, but these raise issues of ownership of those purchases and whether the exchange of money for particular elements of IP is equal to an exchange of IP rights for them. *Pokémon Go* was developed by Niantic, a company spun out of Google, and making use of Google Maps' data, much of which was also submitted by users. The game is an example of an augmented reality game, in which players interact in real spaces with virtual content mapped over them (Nichols 2020). The use of that data as a way to draw players to particular locations has also raised the question of virtual trespass, which asks who owns the virtual spaces that augmented reality games such *Pokémon Go* rely on. While it is unclear whether these areas of contested ownership between players and Nintendo and other game companies will become a problem, it suggests one key area to watch, as it represents an area where there might be challenges to the company and the broader industry.

Patents and Competition

Another area where Nintendo has experienced considerable challenges has been in the area of hardware and patents. With virtually every piece of hardware the company has released, there have been concerns over patent violations. In part, this owes to the company's use of relatively inexpensive, off-the-shelf technologies discussed in Chapter 3. By using fairly simple technologies – sometimes by developing them in-house and sometimes using already developed tech – the company has been able to come up with innovative ways of engaging with its products while also putting itself in competition with a number of developers. But it also can be seen connecting to the company's emphasis on developing new forms of interface to keep their games fresh, such as the 3D interface it used with the Nintendo 3DS handheld console, which resulted in Nintendo having to pay a small royalty on each device sold (Farokhmanesh, 2013; Lien, 2014). As such, Nintendo has been involved several notable suits related to patent disputes (Adkins, 2010).

For example, the company's Wii controller, considered quite innovative, relied on fairly simple technologies which allowed it to track user motion and over the console's interface. But this resulted in at least eight lawsuits between 2008 and 2020 over the tech involved (Bae, 2022). In 2010, the company was sued in U.S. courts over the motion tech, ultimately winning the suit in appeal (Yakowicz, 2017; Lyons, 2020). That same year, another U.S.-based lawsuit was filed about the company's use of particular interface technologies in the

Wii Fit and Wii Balance Boards, in which evidence was shown of the Nintendo seeking out one of the companies involved in developing the technology years prior to releasing the *Wii Fit* and Balance Board. Nintendo would ultimately win that suit as well (Adkins, 2010; Sarkar, 2013).

Though much less successful as a platform, the Wii U also received its share of attention for lawsuits which also focused on the console's interface. The Wii U used touch screen technology and could make use of multiple screens (Farokhmanesh, 2014). Because of the use of that technology, the company was involved in multiple lawsuits. Notably Dutch company Philips sued Nintendo not just in the United States but also in the United Kingdom, Germany, and France. Ultimately, Nintendo settled with the company (Sarkar, 2013). What is perhaps most notable is that while the Wii U was a commercial flop, the technology it used served as a sort of proof-of-concept for the Nintendo Switch, which had similar capabilities and used them to much greater success. The Switch also saw its share of lawsuits, focused on its controls, called JoyCons, and its general design. Again, the company would ultimately prevail, though after several years of legal battles (DeAngelis, 2020).

The use of patents related to platforms has made the question of IP more complex. Because game hardware relies on custom operating systems, a form of software, there can be an interplay between the two different forms of IP: patents for hardware and copyright for software. As discussed previously, Nintendo's use of microchips to control software had previously resulted in the creation of specialized programs to allow non-authorized software on their platforms. More recently, a different use of microchips has been used to allow access to the consoles themselves. These specialized chips essentially unlock the console, allowing users to play unauthorized games, including games which have not been region locked (Widla, 2017). Region locking is a practice common in the games industry as well as in film and recorded music, and other high-tech devices. It is worth noting that some more recent consoles including the Nintendo Switch and Sony's PlayStation 5 do not make use of region locking (Byford, 2017; Peters, 2020). It allows specific software to only be played on devices sold in particular regions of the world. This, in turn, allows for staggered releases across the world as well as content localization – the adaptation of content to a particular location and its customs, laws, and languages (Game Dev Insider, 2021). A 2011 Italian lawsuit between Nintendo and a company named PC Box which sold microchips that would allow users to circumvent the protection on Nintendo's 3DS. Nintendo won the lawsuit, drawing on the EU's InfoSoc directive rather than just its rules on software. This effectively creates a hybrid area of IP law that has been seen to give tremendous amounts of control to hardware manufacturers (Widla, 2017).

A second concern that rises from this is the ability of companies with key patents or control of key platforms to force the development of patent shelters that not only protect their devices and IP but also serve to limit competition (Bagheri et al., 2016). Elements of this can be seen in much of the litigation surrounding Nintendo's various consoles. Indeed, this raises the concern of monopsony by Nintendo or other major players within the games industry. Monopsony is a special form of market concentration that is the flip side of a monopoly. Instead of dominating production, monopsony is domination of a market through consumption. Moreover, concentration in one area often leads to concentration in another (Robinson, 1969). While monopsony is typically examined in terms of labor, it could present in other acts of consumption (Manning, 2003; Nathan, 2021). Specialized microchip development, purchasing in global supply chains, and purchasing and control of IP (as well as consumer data) in high-tech industries, including the games industry, represent likely areas where monopsony would likely be of concern.

Consumer Suits

Consumers, too, have had their issues with Nintendo. Much like the patent lawsuits, most of these have centered around issues with controllers for platforms, though there have been several notable lawsuits concerned with whether Nintendo games caused seizures ("Lawsuits Filed . . ., 2013). The lawsuits focused on controller issues have ranged from individual suits to class-action suits. In the years following the Wii's release, the company faced a number of lawsuits focused on the Wii remotes. Most of the lawsuits focused on problems with straps on Wii remotes. The remotes, which were more wand shaped than typical console controllers allowing them to function in a variety of ways including simulating tennis rackets and other sports equipment, sometimes slipped from users' grips. The suits themselves focused on whether the straps included were defective (Miller, 2006; Dziuban, 2008). The Nintendo Switch also resulted in a number of suits focused on the JoyCon controllers, which frequently experienced what was called "drift" in which the controllers falsely registered movement (DeAngelis, 2020; Chan, 2021). In most cases, these suits have been resolved either through settlement or arbitration, they've not had the impact many of the intra-industry suits have, but they do suggest important challenges to the company as well as offering the rare cases of the company admitting fault, as it did with the Switch JoyCon issues, ultimately apologizing to its fans for the problem (Bae, 2022).

Nintendo and the Environment

One key feature of Nintendo's hardware production process is its use of globalized outsourcing throughout its chain of production. As noted in Chapter 2, Nintendo has largely avoided owning its own factories. Instead, the company has relied on a series of manufacturers and suppliers for its provisions. Video game consoles, like other high-tech devices, rely heavily on a variety of rare minerals in their manufacture (Nichols, 2013, 2014). However, it has become common practice to outsource the purchase of these materials, which allows Nintendo and other game companies to maintain some distance from the problematic nature of conflict minerals (Vick, 2001). So great was the demand for these minerals that at one point pundits began to refer to the war in the Democratic Republic of the Congo as the "Playstation War," though the other major console makers, including Nintendo, as well as most other high-tech devices including computers and smart phones also relied on the minerals produced there and in other conflict zones (Lasker, 2008; Nichols, 2014). Once minerals are procured, and the various components purchases, a majority of console assembly – including Nintendo's – is completed in Southeast Asia (Nichols, 2013; Lam, 2019). Such production allows console manufacturers to take advantage of low labor costs as well as less restrictive workplace and environmental policies. This reliance on problematic procurement of such minerals combined with the issues related to production resulted in considerable criticism of Nintendo and other console manufacturers for poor environmental standards (Greenpeace, 2007; Greenpeace, 2008; Orland 2010). By 2010, Nintendo was rated at the bottom of Greenpeace's report on consumer electronics. Those reports looked at a range of environmental impacts, including the production, recyclability, and energy efficiency of the products being examined (Jenkins, 2010).

Since that time, Nintendo has taken steps to better its environmental record, specifically addressing the issue as a part of its corporate social responsibility initiatives, which included efforts both to make its offices environmentally more efficient as well as closer review and to update its production processes and facilitation of recycling efforts along the product lifecycle (ESG, 2023; Nintendo, 2023). Since the Greenpeace reports, much of the environmental focus has shifted away from concerns along the value chain to focus on environmental concerns about the impact of individual consoles, making it difficult to determine the degree to which Nintendo's range of initiatives are actually effective or whether they're an example of corporate green washing. But while consoles have become increasingly problematic, particularly in terms of their energy requirements, the evidence does point to Nintendo's consoles as working to be more efficient in these regards, with the Switch receiving the highest marks of its console generation (Camacho, 2021; Ellmore, 2021).

Conclusion

With some of the most well-recognized IP in the world, Nintendo has the potential for both incredible cultural and political power. Perhaps the best example of the company's recognition of the importance of its IP has been the moves it has begun to make to move from licensing its properties to other industries discussed previously. Maintaining the value and control of that IP has been one of the chief challenges Nintendo has faced. Despite those challenges, the company has been largely content to wield its power in relatively subtle ways and, whenever possible, within the games industry itself, where it has continued to set standards the rest of the industry has tended to follow. At times, as with the company's acknowledgment of same-sex couples, this has meant pushing against larger social trends. In other cases, as with the company's environmental initiatives, this has meant succumbing to outside pressures. Within the industry, Nintendo's focus on innovative design and interface will continue to be a point of contention with both competitors and companies seeking to develop new technologies. The company will likely face similar challenges with fans and others seeking to capitalize on or make use of popular Nintendo content. The company has walked a particularly difficult line with its fans as it has used litigation to defend its IP, but it has largely been successful in doing so even as the company has developed a reputation for being particularly litigious. Not surprisingly, this means that Nintendo and its products are likely candidates for relatively unexplored concerns in the games industry, including virtual trespass, ownership of digital purchases, and monopsony. Despite the company's small size, it is clear that Nintendo will continue to be found at the center of issues that impact not just the video game industry but also a range of high-tech concerns.

Notes

1 Tables 4.2 and 4.3 attempt to break out Nintendo anime in terms of whether the text in question is feature length, defined here as 60 minutes or longer. Anime that is feature length was placed with feature films and other items in Table 4.2, while shorter anime and serialized examples were grouped with information on television shows.
2 "Gotta catch 'em all!" is the trade-marked marketing slogan associated with Pokémon.

References

100 Million (Pirated) Nintendo Games in China. (1995). *Consumer Electronics, 1.*
A Brief History of All Things Mean Machine. (2019, November 17). Mean Machines Archive. https://web.archive.org/web/20191117140638/http://www.meanmachines-mag.co.uk/history.php
Adkins, J. L. (2010). A Review of 2010 Video Game Litigation and Selected Cases. *SMU Science & Technology Law Review, 14,* 439.
The Adventures of Super Mario Bros. 3. (2023). [Animation, Adventure, Comedy]. *IMDB.com.*
Akhtar, A. (2016, July 13). Holocaust Museum, Auschwitz want Pokémon Go Hunts Out. *USA Today.*
Amada Anime Series: Super Mario. (2023). [Animation, Short, Adventure]. *IMDB.com.* https://www.imdb.com/title/tt3336822/?ref_=nv_sr_srsg_0
AP. (1989, February 2). Nintendo is Sued by Atari. *The New York Times.* https://www.nytimes.com/1989/02/02/business/nintendo-is-sued-by-atari.html
AusReprints. (2023). AusReprints – Nintendo Magazine System (Trielle Corporation, 1993 Series). *AusReprints.net.* https://ausreprints.net/series/8043/0
Bae, C.M. (2022, September 11). Why Multiple Companies Sued Nintendo Over the Wii. *SVG.* https://www.svg.com/1003029/why-multiple-companies-sued-nintendo-over-the-wii/
Bagheri, S. K., Minin, A. D., Paraboschi, A., & Piccaluga, A. (2016). It's Not about Being Generous: Platform Leaders and Patent Shelters. *Research-Technology Management, 59*(2), 28–35.

Beer, S. (2008, November 12). *iTWire – New Official Nintendo Magazine Launched in ANZ.* https://itwire.com/it-industry-news/strategy/21647-new-official-nintendo-magazine-launched-in-anz

Box Office Mojo. (2023). Franchise: Pokémon. *Box Office Mojo.* https://www.boxofficemojo.com/franchise/fr2907148037/

A Brief History of All Things Mean Machine. (2019, November 17). *Mean Machines Archive.* https://web.archive.org/web/20191117140638/http://www.meanmachinesmag.co.uk/history.php

Buckley, S. (2016). Nintendo Issues DMCA Takedown for Hundreds of Fan Games. *Engadget.*

Byford, S. (2017, March 9). The Secret best Nintendo Switch Feature is Its Lack of Region-Locking. *The Verge.* https://www.theverge.com/2017/3/9/14867076/nintendo-switch-no-region-locking-awesome

Camacho, R. (2021, February 23). Nintendo Switch is Most Eco-Friendly Console, Study Finds. *Game Rant.* https://gamerant.com/nintendo-switch-eco-friendly-console-study-finds/

Captain N: The Game Master. (2023). [Animation, Action, Adventure]. *IMDB.com.* https://www.imdb.com/title/tt0096554/?ref_=nv_sr_srsg_0

Carpenter, N. (2021, June 1). Nintendo Awarded $2.1M in Pirated Games Lawsuit. *Polygon.* https://www.polygon.com/22462914/nintendo-lawsuit-2-million-damages-rom-universe-pirated-games

Chan, K. H. (2021, December 14). Here's a Snapshot of Nintendo's Convoluted Legal History. *TheGamer.* https://www.thegamer.com/a-snapshot-of-nintendos-convoluted-legal-history/

Chowdhry, A. (2015, January 20). Club Nintendo is Shutting Down, But a New Loyalty Program Is Coming. *Forbes.* https://www.forbes.com/sites/amitchowdhry/2015/01/20/club-nintendo-shutting-down/

Cifaldi, F. (2012, December 11). Nintendo Power: Remembering America's Longest-Lasting Game Magazine. *Game Developer.* https://www.gamedeveloper.com/business/nintendo-power-remembering-america-s-longest-lasting-game-magazine

Coates, J. (1993, May 17). How Super Mario Conquered America. *Baltimore Sun.* https://www.baltimoresun.com/news/bs-xpm-1993-05-18-1993138174-story.html

Commission Fines Nintendo for Anti-Trust Violations. (2002, October 30). *Pinsent Masons.* https://www.pinsentmasons.com/out-law/news/commission-fines-nintendo-for-anti-trust-violations

Dark Horse. (2023). *Super Mario Encyclopedia: The Official Guide to the First 30 Years HC: Profile: Dark Horse Comics.* https://www.darkhorse.com/Books/30-956/Super-Mario-Encyclopedia-The-Official-Guide-to-the-First-30-Years-HC

DeAngelis, M. (2020, March 13). Nintendo Prevails in Lawsuit Over Switch Console and JoyCon Design. *Engadget.* https://www.engadget.com/2020-03-13-nintendo-wins-gamevice-lawsuit.html

Dengeki Nintendo Magazine to Launch in April. (2023, April 13). *Anime News Network.* https://www.animenewsnetwork.com/interest/2013-03-18/dengeki-nintendo-magazine-to-launch-in-april

Donkey Kong Country. (2023). [Animation, Action, Adventure]. *IMDB.com.* https://www.imdb.com/title/tt0149447/?ref_=nv_sr_srsg_1

Dziuban, L. J. (2008, December 12). Nintendo Faces Class-Action Lawsuit, Hotter-than-Ever Sales for Wii. *Engadget.* https://www.engadget.com/2008-12-12-nintendo-faces-class-action-lawsuit-hotter-than-ever-sales-for.html

Ellmore, J. (2021, October 14). The Lifetime Cost of a Gaming Console: PS5 vs Xbox Series X|S. *NerdWallet UK.* https://www.nerdwallet.com/uk/personal-finance/game-console-total-cost-of-ownership/

ESAC. (2019, October 22). *About ESAC – Entertainment Software Association of Canada.* Entertainment Software Association of Canada. https://theesa.ca/about/about-esac/

ESG. (2023, January 4). Nintendo Addresses Environmental Issues in Latest Report | ESG Review. *ESG Review.* https://esgreview.net/2023/01/04/nintendo-addresses-environmental-issues-in-latest-report/

The Fabulous History of Pokémon. (1999, October 10). The Salt Lake Tribune. *ProQuest Newsstand,* J1.

Faia emuburemu. (2023). [Animation, Action, Adventure]. *IMDB.com.* https://www.imdb.com/title/tt0332056/?ref_=fn_al_tt_1

Farokhmanesh, M. (2013, February 27). Nintendo Being Sued for 3D Patent Infringement. *Polygon.* https://www.polygon.com/2013/2/27/4036520/nintendo-being-sued-for-3d-patent-infringement

Farokhmanesh, M. (2014, April 17). Nintendo Engaged in Lawsuit Over Alleged Wii U Patent Infringement. *Polygon.* https://www.polygon.com/2014/4/17/5624886/Nintendo-lawsuit-wii-u-patent-infringement

Figueroa, S. (2018, December 14). Cierra la Revista Oficial Nintendo, se acabó Nintendo Acción. *Gamereactor España.* https://www.gamereactor.es/cierra-la-revista-oficial-nintendo-se-acabo-nintendo-accion/

Ford, W. K. (2012). Copy Game for High Score: The First Video Game Lawsuit. *Journal of Intellectual Property Law, 20,* 1.

Forman, E. (1989). *Nintendo Steps Up Blockbuster Battle: Sun* (Sentinel ed.). Sun-Sentinel (Fort Lauderdale, Fla.).

Future International Licensing. (2008, November 11). https://web.archive.org/web/20081111133014/http://www.futurelicensing.com/home/titles/WII

Future PLC. (2023). *Home to the World's Most Popular Brands.* Future PLC. https://www.futureplc.com/our-brands/

Future Publishing. (2023). *Magazines from the Past Wiki.* https://magazinesfromthepast.fandom.com/wiki/Future_Publishing

F-Zero GP Legend. (2023). [Animation, Action, Adventure]. *IMDB.com.* https://www.imdb.com/title/tt0433289/?ref_=nv_sr_srsg_1

Gaines, J. (2016, October 11). Where Have All the Magazines Gone? | Librarypoint. *LIbraryPoint.org.* https://web.archive.org/web/20161011145110/http://www.library-point.org/where_have_all_the_magazines_gone

Game Dev Insider. (2021, May 27). Why Are Games Region Locked? *Game Dev Insider.* https://gamedevinsider.com/why-are-games-region-locked/

GamesRadar. (2012, January 5). NGamer, the UK's Only Independent Nintendo Magazine, is Relaunched Today as Nintendo Gamer. *Gamesradar.* https://www.gamesradar.com/ngamer-uks-only-independent-nintendo-magazine-relaunched-today-nintendo-gamer/

Gaudiosi, J. (2005). China Caught in Web of Games: Report Finds Most of Sector Revenue Comes from Online Activity. *Hollywood Reporter, 388*(33), 16.

Gekijô-ban Dôbutsu no Mori. (2023). [Animation, Comedy, Drama]. *IMDB.com.* https://www.imdb.com/title/tt1190545/?ref_=fn_al_tt_1

Gekijô-ban poketto monsutâ– Myûtsû no gyakushû. (2023). [Animation, Action, Adventure]. *IMDB.com.* https://www.imdb.com/title/tt0190641/?ref_=nv_sr_srsg_6

Gonzalez, J. M. (2012, September 28). Historia de las revistas de juegos en España. *Vandal.elespanol.com.* https://vandal.elespanol.com/reportaje/historia-de-las-revistas-de-juegos-en-espana

Good, O. S. (2023, April 18). Bowser Released from Prison, Still Has to Pay Nintendo $10 Million. *Polygon.* https://www.polygon.com/23688170/gary-bowser-hacker-nintendo-released-restitution

Greenpeace. (2007, November 27). *Nintendo, Microsoft and Phillips Flunk Toxic Test.* http://www.greenpeace.org/international/en/news/features/greener-electronics-ranking-6-291107/

Greenpeace. (2008, May 20). *Game Consoles: No Consolation.* http://www.greenpeace.org/international/en/news/features/game-consoles-no-consolation200508/

Herranz, S. (2018, December 14). Cierra la histórica Nintendo Acción. *Hobbyconsolas.* https://www.hobbyconsolas.com/noticias/cierra-historica-nintendo-accion-345735

Holland, T. (Director). (1989, June 30). *The Wizard* [Adventure, Comedy, Drama]. Carolco Pictures, Finnegan/Pinchuk Productions, Pipeline Productions.

Hrin, B. (2017, November 30). [Industry Interviews] Paul Murphy from Switch Player Magazine. *The Switch Effect.* http://theswitcheffect.net/2017/11/industry-interviews-paul-murphy-from-switch-player-magazine/

Intervista a Raffaele Sogni. (n.d.). Digilander. *Libero.it.* Retrieved April 13, 2023, from https://digilander.libero.it/mariomagazine/intervista-raffo.html

ISFE. (2023). *Our Membership.* Interactive Software Federation of Europe. https://www.isfe.eu/our-membership/

Issuu. (n.d.). *About Issuu – Connecting Content to People.* Issuu. Retrieved April 13, 2023, from https://issuu.com/about

Jenkins, D. (2007, February 26). Japanese Government Sells Nintendo Shares. *Game Developer.* https://www.gamedeveloper.com/console/japanese-government-sells-nintendo-shares

Jenkins, D. (2010, May 28). Nintendo Still Least Greenpeace-Friendly Company | GamesIndustry.biz. *GamesIndustry.biz.* https://www.gamesindustry.biz/nintendo-still-least-greenpeace-friendly-company

Jenkins, H. (2006). *Convergence Culture: Where Old Media and New Media Collide.* New York: Routledge.

Johnson, D. (2013). *Media Franchising: Creative License and Collaboration in the Culture Industries.* NYU Press. https://doi.org/10.18574/9780814743492

Jurkovich, T. (2021, February 9). The 15 Best Selling Nintendo Franchises of All Time, Ranked. *TheGamer.* https://www.thegamer.com/nintendo-best-selling-franchises-all-time/

Kharpal, A. (2022, December 7). Microsoft Says It Will Bring Call of Duty to Nintendo for 10 Years if Activision Deal Closes. *CNBC.* https://www.cnbc.com/2022/12/07/microsoft-says-it-will-bring-call-of-duty-to-nintendo-for-10-years.html

King Koopa's Kool Kartoons. (2023). [Family]. *IMDB.com.* https://www.imdb.com/title/tt2724702/?ref_=nv_sr_srsg_0

Kirby: Right Back at Ya! (2023). [Animation, Action, Adventure]. *IMDB.com.* https://www.imdb.com/title/tt0338621/?ref_=fn_al_tt_1

Knight, R. (2022, April 1). Every Nintendo Cartoon, Ranked. *CINEMABLEND.* https://www.cinemablend.com/television/every-nintendo-cartoon-ranked

Kumar, N. (2014, February 26). Shareholder Pushes Nintendo to Join Mobile Gaming Race. *Reuters.* https://www.reuters.com/article/uk-nintendo-hedgefunds-idUKBREA1P0IU20140226

Kurland, D. (2021, June 4). F-Zero & 9 Other Nintendo Games You Didn't Know Had Anime Adaptations. *CBR*. https://www.cbr.com/nintendo-games-anime-adaptations-little-known/

Lam, A. (2019, December 4). Nintendo Switch Life Cycle. *Design Life-Cycle*. http://www.designlife-cycle.com/nintendo-switch

Lasker, J. (2008, July 8). Inside Africa's PlayStation War. *Toward Freedom*. https://towardfreedom.org/story/archives/africa-archives/inside-africas-playstation-war/

Lawsuits Filed after Games Caused Seizures. (2013, April 6). *Seizures from Video Games*. https://videogameseizures.wordpress.com/2013/04/06/lawsuits-filed-after-games-caused-seizures/

Lee, C. A. (2022). Video Game Modding in the U.S. Intellectual Property Law: Controversial Issues and Gaps. *Digital Law Journal*, *3*(4), 8–31. https://doi.org/10.38044/2686-9136-2022-3-4-8-31

Letterman, R. (Director). (2019, May 10). *Pokémon: Detective Pikachu* [Action, Adventure, Comedy]. Warner Bros, Legendary Entertainment, The Pokémon Company.

Lien, T. (2014, January 6). Nintendo to Pay Royalties Over 3DS Patent Infringement. *Polygon*. https://www.polygon.com/2014/1/6/5281228/nintendo-to-pay-royalties-over-3ds-patent-infringement

List of Television Series and Films. (2023, March 8). *Super Mario Wiki*. https://www.mariowiki.com/List_of_television_series_and_films

Lunney, G. S. Jr. (1989). Atari Games v. Nintendo: Does a Closed System Violate the Antitrust Laws. *High Technology Letters Journal*, *5*, 29.

Lyons, K. (2020, January 21). A Company that Sued Nintendo for Patent Violation Didn't Actually Invent Anything, Judge Rules. *The Verge*. https://www.theverge.com/2020/1/21/21075799/nintendo-wii-remote-wiimote-patent-case-verdict-ilife-lawsuit

MacLean, P. A. (1991, January 8). Nintendo Hit with $105 Million Antitrust Suit by American Video – UPI Archives. *UPI*. https://www.upi.com/Archives/1991/01/08/Nintendo-hit-with-105-million-antitrust-suit-by-American-Video/3242663310800/

Manning, A. (2003). *Monopsony in Motion: Imperfect Competition in Labor Markets*. Princeton, NJ: Princeton University Press.

Martin, G. (2021, November 8). The 10 Best-Selling Nintendo Franchises of All Time. *Pastemagazine.com*. https://www.pastemagazine.com/games/nintendo/best-selling-nintendo-franchises/

McFerran, D. (2011, August 5). The Making of TOTAL! Magazine. *Nintendo Life*. https://www.nintendolife.com/news/2011/08/feature_the_making_of_total_magazine

MCV. (2012, August 30). Future Closes Nintendo Gamer. *MCV*. https://www.mcvuk.com/business-news/future-closes-nintendo-gamer/

Miller, P. (2006, December 19). Nintendo Hit with Class Action Lawsuit for "Defective" Wrist Straps. *Engadget*. https://www.engadget.com/2006-12-19-nintendo-hit-with-class-action-lawsuit-for-defective-wrist-str.html

Mitchell, R. (2016). Pokémon Go-es Directly to Court: How Pokémon Go Illustrates the Issue of Virtual Trespass and the Need for Evolved Tort Laws. *Texas Tech Law Review*, *49*, 959.

Mochizuki, T., & Furukawa, Y. (2023, February 17). Saudi Arabia Becomes Largest Outside Shareholder of Nintendo. *Bloomberg.com*. https://www.bloomberg.com/news/articles/2023-02-17/saudi-arabia-becomes-largest-outside-shareholder-of-nintendo

Nakanishi, T. (2003). Nintendo Takes Game War to China. *The Nikkei Weekly (Japan)*. NexisUni.

Nathan, D. (2021). From Monopoly to Monopsony Capitalism. *Indian Journal of Labour Economics, 64*(4), 843–866. https://doi.org/10.1007/s41027-021-00350-w

Nations of the World Confront the Pokémon Menace. (2016, July 22). *The Business Times*.

Nichols, R. (2013). Who Plays, Who Pays? Mapping Video Game Production and Consumption Globally. In N. B. Huntemann & B. Aslinger (Eds.), *Gaming Globally: Production, Play and Place* (pp. 19–39). New York: Palgrave MacMillan.

Nichols, R. (2014). *The Video Game Business (International Screen Industries)*. New York, NY: Palgrave Macmillan on Behalf of the British Film Institute.

Nichols, R. (2020). Pokémon Go: Globalization. In M. T. Payne & N. B. Huntemann (Eds.), *How to Play Video Games* (pp. 250–258). New York, USA: New York University Press. https://doi.org/10.18574/9781479830404-032

Nintendo. (2015, January 20). Important Information about the Discontinuation of Club Nintendo. *Nintendo of Europe GmbH*. https://www.nintendo.co.uk/News/2015/January/Important-information-about-the-discontinuation-of-Club-Nintendo-949921.html

Nintendo. (2023). Environment. *Nintendo.com*. https://www.nintendo.com/about/csr/environment/

Nintendo and Future US Team To Publish Nintendo Power Magazine Future US, Inc. (2013, November 2). https://web.archive.org/web/20131102071200/http://www.futureus.com/2007/09/19/nintendo-and-future-us-team-to-publish-nintendo-power-magazine/

Nintendo Rivista Ufficiale. (n.d.). *Nintendo of Europe GmbH*. Retrieved April 13, 2023, from https://www.nintendo.it/Altro/Nintendo-Rivista-Ufficiale-773791.html

Nintendo to Make, Sell Games in China. (1993). *The Nikkei Weekly (Japan)*. NexisUni.

Nintendomagasinet (1990) – Visa katalogvärde och omslag till serietidningar och album. (2023). *Seriesams Guide*. https://www.seriesam.com/cgi-bin/guide?s=Nintendomaga sinet+(1990)

Official Nintendo Magazine Celebrates 100 Issues! (2013, April 10). *Nintendo of Europe GmbH*. https://www.nintendo.co.uk/News/2013/October/Official-Nintendo-Magazine-celebrates-100-issues--814337.html

Olney, N. (2014, December 23). Nintendo Invests in New Lobbying Firm to Tackle Piracy of Intellectual Property. *Nintendo Life*. https://www.nintendolife.com/news/2014/12/nintendo_invests_in_new_lobbying_firm_to_tackle_piracy_of_intellectual_property

ONM. (2014, October 7). Official Nintendo Magazine Set to Close with Issue 114 – Official Nintendo Magazine. *Official Nintendo Magazine UK*. https://web.archive.org/web/20141007181333/http://www.officialnintendomagazine.co.uk/58338/official-nintendo-magazine-set-to-close-with-issue-114/

Orland, K. (2010, October 26). *Greenpeace Criticizes Nintendo and Microsoft's Environmental Records*. http://www.gamasutra.com/view/news/31174/Greenpeace_Criticizes_Nintendo_and_Microsofts_Environmental_Records.php

Orland, K. (2016). Nintendo's DMCA-Backed Quest Against Online Fan Games. *ArsTechnica.com*.

Patterson, A. (2018, May 4). Random House Imprint to Publish Children's Books Based on Nintendo Characters and Worlds. *Paste Magazine*. https://www.pastemagazine.com/books/nintendo/random-house-to-publish-childrens-books-based-on-n

Payne, M. T. (2019). "Now They're Playing with Power!": Nintendo's Classics and Franchise Legacy Management. In J. Fleury, B. Hikari Harzheim, & S. Mamber (Eds.), *The*

Franchise Era: Managing Media in the Digital Economy (pp. 105–118). Edinburgh: Edinburgh University Press.

Perlmutter, D. (2014). *America Toons In: A History of Television Animation*. Jefferson, NC: McFarland & Company, Incorporated Publishers.

Peters, J. (2020, November 9). Sony Reveals PS5 Games Will be Region Free, and the Console Will Support PS Now. *The Verge*. https://www.theverge.com/2020/11/9/21556760/ ps5-sony-playstation-5-region-free-ps-now-support

Plunkett, L. (2012, August 22). Remembering Nintendo's Other 1980's Magazine, The Nintendo Fun Club. *Kotaku*. https://kotaku.com/remembering-nintendos-other-1980s-magazine-the-nintend-5936766

Pokémon. (2023). [Animation, Action, Adventure]. *IMDB.com*. https://www.imdb.com/ title/tt0168366/?ref_=nv_sr_srsg_0

Pokémon Journeys. (2023). [Animation, Adventure, Comedy]. *IMDB.com*. https://www. imdb.com/title/tt14033496/?ref_=nv_sr_srsg_7

Pokémon Mania Near Holy Kaaba Slammed. (2016, July 28). *TCA Regional News*.

Pokémon Master Journeys (TV Series 2021) – Company Credits – IMDb. (2023). *IMDB. com*. https://www.imdb.com/title/tt15416672/companycredits/

Porter, R. (2020, April 23). Netflix Snags Rights to "Pokémon" Animated Series. *The Hollywood Reporter*. https://www.hollywoodreporter.com/tv/tv-news/netflix-snags-rights-pok-mon-animated-series-1291470/

Rakuten.com. (2012, October 29). *2007年度興行成績ランキング＜映画―楽天エンタ メナビ*. https://web.archive.org/web/20121029165113/; http://entertainment.rakuten. co.jp/movie/ranking/boxoffice/2007/

Razak, M. (2010, January 24). Microsoft Cites Nintendo and Apple in Antitrust Case. *Destructoid*. https://www.destructoid.com/microsoft-cites-nintendo-and-apple-in-antitrust-case/

Robinson, J. (1969). *The Economics of Imperfect Competition* (2nd ed.). London: Palgrave Macmillan.

Rossow, A. L. (2016). Gotta Catch a Lawsuit: A Legal Insight into the Intellectual, Civil, and Criminal Battlefield Pokémon Go Has Downloaded onto Smartphones and Properties Around the World. *John Marshall Review of Intellectual Property Law, 16*(3), [i]–349.

Rougeau, M. (n.d.). New Magazine "Nintendo Force" Aims to Continue the "Nintendo Power" Legacy. *Complex*. Retrieved April 13, 2023, from https://www. complex.com/pop-culture/2012/12/new-magazine-nintendo-force-aims-to-continue-the-nintendo-power-legacy

Santucci, S. (2023). *Entertainment Software Association | About The ESA*. Entertainment Software Association. https://www.theesa.com/about-esa/

Sarkar, S. (2013, June 19). Federal Court Upholds Nintendo's Victory in Wii Fit Patent Lawsuit. *Polygon*. https://www.polygon.com/2013/6/19/4445974/ wii-fit-patent-lawsuit-nintendo-ia-labs-ruling-upheld

Saturday Supercade. (2023). [Animation, Family, Adventure]. *IMDB.com*. https://www. imdb.com/title/tt0085008/?ref_=fn_al_tt_1

Scullion, C. (2012, September 2). Nintendo Gamer Magazine to Close | Nintendo Gamer. *Nintendo Gamer.net*. https://web.archive.org/web/20120902052848/http://www. nintendo-gamer.net/2012/08/30/nintendo-gamer-magazine-to-close/

Sheff, D. (1993). *Game Over: How Nintendo Zapped an American Industry, Captured Your Dollars, and Enslaved Your Children*. New York, NY: Random House.

Shimada, M. (2019). Nintendo v. MariCar: Is Street Kart Rental Business Free Riding on the Popular Video Game Characters Prohibited in Japan? *Interactive Entertainment Law Review, 2*(1), 50–54. https://doi.org/10.4337/ielr.2019.01.05

Shishkin, P. (2002, October 25). Europe Decides to Fine Nintendo – Antitrust Enforcers Rule That the Videogame Maker Illegally Carved Up Market. *Wall Street Journal*, B5.

Simon & Schuster. (2023). *Nintendo*. Simon & Schuster. https://www.simonandschuster.com/authors/Nintendo/171577341

Skrebels, J. (2021, July 30). Nintendo Reportedly Pulled Out of the Olympics Opening Ceremony. *IGN*. https://www.ign.com/articles/nintendo-olympics-opening-ceremony

Stanglin, D. (2016). Fatwa No. 21,758: Saudi clerics ban Pokémon Go. *USA Today*.

Steve Jarratt Interview. (n.d.). *Out of Print Archive.com*. Retrieved April 13, 2023, from http://www.outofprintarchive.com/articles/interviews/out-of-print/Steve_Jarratt_interview.html

Stuart, K. (2018, March 22). "The Stench of It Stays with Everybody": Inside the Super Mario Bros. Movie. *The Guardian*. https://www.theguardian.com/games/2018/mar/22/super-mario-bros-movie-killing-fields-chariots-fire-video-game

Sûpâ Mario burazâzu: Pîchi-hime kyushutsu dai sakusen! (2023). [Animation, Adventure, Comedy]. *IMDB.com*. https://www.imdb.com/title/tt0469611/?ref_=nv_sr_srsg_0

Super Mario All-Stars. (2023). [Action, Adventure, Family]. *IMDB.com*. https://www.imdb.com/title/tt0221603/?ref_=nv_sr_srsg_0

The Super Mario Bros. Super Show! (2023). [Animation, Action, Adventure]. *IMDB.com*. https://www.imdb.com/title/tt0096707/?ref_=fn_al_tt_1

The Super Mario Challenge. (2023). [Family]. *IMDB.com*. https://www.imdb.com/title/tt4241626/?ref_=nv_sr_srsg_0

Super Mario World. (2023). [Animation, Adventure, Comedy]. *IMDB.com*. https://www.imdb.com/title/tt0167552/?ref_=nv_sr_srsg_7

Ulysse 31. (2023). [Animation, Action, Adventure]. *IMDB.com*. https://www.imdb.com/title/tt0131190/

Van Hassteren, A., & Peña Castellot, M. (2002, October 30). *Commission Fines Nintendo and Seven of Its European Distributors for Colluding to Prevent Trade in Low-Priced Products*. European Commission. https://ec.europa.eu/competition/publications/cpn/2003_1_50.pdf

Vick, K. (2001). Vital Ore Funds Congo's War; Combatants Profit from Col-Tan Trade. *The Washington Post*, 0-A.1. ProQuest Central.

Wallace, R. (2014). Modding: Amateur Authorship and How the Video Game Industry is Actually Getting It Right. *Brigham Young University Law Review, 2014*(1), 219.

Weber, J. (1992, May 2). Jury Sides with Nintendo in Suit Brought by Atari. *The Los Angeles Times*.

Widla, B. (2017). More than a Game: Did Nintendo v. PC Box Give Manufacturers More Control Over the Use of Hardware? *The Computer Law and Security Report, 33*(2), 242–249. https://doi.org/10.1016/j.clsr.2016.11.013

Wikipedia. (2022, October 1). *Nintendo World*. Wikipedia. https://en.wikipedia.org/w/index.php?title=Nintendo_World&oldid=1113347488

Wikipedia. (2023a, January 24). *Pure Nintendo Magazine*. Wikipedia. https://en.wikipedia.org/w/index.php?title=Pure_Nintendo_Magazine&oldid=1135395592

Wikipedia. (2023b, February 6). *Super Play (Sweden)*. Wikipedia. https://en.wikipedia.org/w/index.php?title=Super_Play_(Sweden)&oldid=1137726879

Yakowicz, W. (2017, September 5). Nintendo Loses Patent Lawsuit, Ordered to Pay $10 Million. *Inc.com*. https://www.inc.com/will-yakowicz/nintendo-loses-patent-infringement-case-wii.html

5   Conclusion

Although Nintendo has never been the largest company in the video game industry, it has been one of the key players since the 1980s. The company's reach demands that it be understood as more than just a producer of toys and entertainment, with an audience that is much broader than just children. Since the company's venture into video games in the 1980s, Nintendo has been vital to the industry's function and legitimization. With its reach into all the major sectors of the industry – software development, software publishing, and hardware manufacturing – the company has helped the industry's structure to stabilize. Moreover, the company's focus on cultivating audiences who would engage with its products over the course of their lifetime, has helped Nintendo extend the reach and importance of the larger industry. Along the way, this meant a change in where and how video games were played and, eventually, in just how popular they would become internationally (Kocurek, 2015; Nichols, 2014). It is a company with both important political reach and cultural impact that extend globally. Understanding the history and development of Nintendo provides key insights into how the video game industry itself works. In part, this is because Nintendo has, over its history, established many of the norms the industry follows. Throughout its more than century-long history, Nintendo has reinvented itself multiple times, adapting to an increasingly globalized world, but with the clear knowledge that the products and services it provides weren't necessities. That knowledge combined with the company's narrow focus of production resulted in a variety of important strategies that distinguish it as a global media giant. Those strategies, in turn, have allowed the company to survive a number of downturns, only to come back stronger.

Nintendo and the Modern Video Game Industry

By 2023, Nintendo was again at the top of its industry. The Switch console was nearing the end of its lifecycle, though the company's replacement console wasn't due for at least another year (Mui, 2023). But the console had been incredibly popular, with software and hardware sales earning more than U.S. $69 billion in the seven years since its release. Estimates suggest that

DOI: 10.4324/9781003031918-5

these sales accounted for more than 90 percent of the company's revenue in that time period (Taylor-Hill, 2023). In addition, the company's popular game series The Legend of Zelda saw the newest release *The Legend of Zelda: Tears of the Kingdom* hit the market in May 2023, a sequel to another popular Switch game, *The Legend of Zelda: Breath of the Wild*, which was released just a few years prior (MacDonald, 2023). Both games proved tremendously popular. At one point, more copies of *Breath of the Wild* had been sold than there were machines capable of playing the game, while *Tears of the Kingdom* had the second-best release of any game in the United Kingdom and sold more than 500,000 copies in France in its first week (Lewellyn, 2023; Dring, 2023; D'Angelo, 2023). Meanwhile, the company's new movie based on the Mario franchise, *The Super Mario Bros. Movie*, earned more than U.S. $1.2 billion globally in just over a month in theaters, making it one of the highest grossing animated films of all time (Malhotra, 2023). Finally, Comcast Corporation announced that its Universal Parks division, which feature the newly developed Super Nintendo World, had seen a 25 percent revenue growth (Friedman, 2023).

While Nintendo certainly isn't new to success, the combination of these is important because it marks several strategic changes on the part of the company. The company, long resistant to extending itself beyond video games, took steps to integrate both into film and theme parks, and it seems likely that the successes in both areas will encourage further experiments. Both the partnership with Illumination and the company's purchase of its own film studio suggests the company is finally interested in becoming a more certain integrated media giant, no longer content to live or die on game sales alone. But that likely means the company will need to adjust some of its long-held practices, particularly its size and handling of cash reserves. At the same time, these expansions and successes did little to disrupt both social and industrial dynamics or the company's responses to them. When images from *Tears of the Kingdom* were released prior to the game's release, Nintendo's concerns about piracy and responses to it were quick and in keeping with the company's established practices: takedown notices using the U.S. Digital Millennium Copyright Act to both Discord and software emulation servers (Gould, 2023; Litchfield, 2023).

Even with such changes, it is clear that while clearly a global media giant, Nintendo has done so in a way which often runs counter to even its closest competitors Sony and Microsoft. While much of the business literature is content to discuss Nintendo's innovation with its most recent consoles, that tendency is one that's been there since the company's first forays into electronic toys, carrying over into the development of video games. Nor is the company necessarily dissuaded by an early failure. Much has been made of the failures of the Wii U console, which was clearly a commercial failure for the company, but little has been said about the ways in which it paved the way for features, such as the use of touch screens and the ability to interface with a television, which made the Switch particularly popular.

Similarly, it becomes clear that while many analysts still see Nintendo as a company focused on video games hardware, that software is at least as central, of not more so, to the company's success. Indeed, to understand Nintendo or the video game industry, it is necessary to think about the relationship between hardware and software and to pay better attention to the production of both (Nichols, 2011). As discussed in previous chapters, Nintendo has taken a different approach to software than its main rivals. Rather than purchasing its own studios and relying on external developers, Nintendo has developed an intensive partnership and licensing system that has served it well since its introduction in the 1980s. At that point, Nintendo's approach was simultaneously seen as saving the industry and creating particularly problematic antitrust concerns. But the company largely won through the litigation on antitrust, and many of its licensing practices became essentially industry standards. That has allowed the company to focus its energies on developing both innovative ways to both keep experiences with its products fun even as it expands what that engagement looks like and who its products engage. In turn, this has made it more difficult for the industry's oligopoly structure to change. While some key players change, Nintendo, Sony, and Microsoft have stayed at the center since the start of the 21st century largely by continuing these patterns.

The question of "who" the company targets with its products is key. Video games have often been treated as entertainment just for children, and certainly Nintendo has played a part in that. But the company has been particularly mindful that it needs both the new gamer audiences that comes with kids and the long-term audience that a company might cultivate. But Nintendo has also worked to develop even outside those lines. When it was developing the Nintendo Wii, one of the company's goals was to design a console that the whole family, particularly parents and grandparents, might want to play. That goal has carried over to subsequent consoles and contributed to their success, particularly the Switch. As with many of the other strategies the company has followed, working to expand audiences helped to benefit and shape the modern video game industry, extending the industry's reach into other areas of cultural production.

Nintendo, too, maintains a globalized production chain. Unlike its rivals, the company has been reluctant to assemble its own consoles, and instead has outsourced most of its hardware production. This has had the dual benefit of cheapening costs and providing some distance from concerns over labor and environmental conditions. But it has also meant the company has been subject to supply chain issues and to concerns over the ways in which it has used its dominance in the industry to its advantage in purchasing goods and services necessary for the production of its products. A deeper examination of these issues is made challenging by the range of networks these production arrangements involve, but given concerns over how supply chains reinforce problematic patterns, such examinations seem all the more vital (Tomaselli et al., 2008; Kelly et al., 2021).

Intellectual Property as a Key Site of Production and Influence

The role of intellectual property (IP) is particularly crucial for understanding Nintendo. As Payne (2019) has argued, Nintendo's tight control over IP has been a double-edged sword. Tight control of Nintendo's IP has allowed the company great success in maintaining high-quality products, something which was vital in the company's earliest days in the video game industry. But it also resulted in significant litigation, and has been an issue for some investors, who have seen the company as too reluctant to expand into new markets like mobile gaming or to capitalize more fully on the licensing possibilities beyond games. The company has begun to make more moves to explore these areas, as seen in its allowing the creation of games like *Pokémon Go* as well as its moves into creating the Super Nintendo World theme parks with Universal Studios. *Pokémon Go* is a particularly useful example as it not only involved work with important partners to develop but also demonstrated ways in which the company and its products had both political and cultural impact (Nichols, 2020).

Indeed, it is through the use and production of its products and the litigation that has surrounded them that Nintendo's political impact can be best understood. Since its first days in the video game industry, the company has been a magnet for litigation over both its business practices and for control of key patents. In turn, Nintendo has used the courts aggressively to protect its IP, using favorable laws in key markets against competitors, pirates, and sometimes even against the fans of its products. While much of Nintendo's hardware production is notable for its use of relatively affordable, off-the-shelf parts used in innovative ways as seen with the Wii console, with each of its consoles in the 21st century the company has been embroiled in patent lawsuits. Though it has largely prevailed, it does raise the question of how control of patents and other IP within high-tech industries like the video games continues to be a key mechanism for maintaining control.

How the company has allowed its IP to be used is a crucial area to watch going forward. While the company's moves to expand into film and theme parks suggest some moves toward integration, Nintendo has still shown some hesitancy about how and where its brands are deployed, as was seen with the example Tokyo Olympics. The company has also been hesitant to release older games, despite how much demand there is. This has resulted in repeated attempts at releasing emulations of those games, something that has meant Nintendo frequently has to take not just large-scale piracy operations to court but often fans as well. While this doesn't seem to have impacted fan perception of the company, that is an area that can change quickly.

Nintendo Looking Forward

While Nintendo might have seemed an unlikely global media giant, it has clearly secured its place in that group. As it goes forward, it faces a number of key challenges. First, though the market for games is expanding, how and where that expansion is occurring is something the company will need to address. Though Nintendo has made some inroads in mobile gaming, it has largely been focused on its own platforms. And like the rest of the industry, as gaming markets grow to focus on areas outside of the Global North, this will require rethinking both content and access issues to accommodate cultures and infrastructures distinct from the company's current primary markets. Perhaps this will be addressed as the company thinks about the console that will follow the wildly popular Nintendo Switch. Addressing these needs might also help the company with its ongoing struggle with piracy. The partnerships the company has attempted to forge in China and other areas will be vital for this going forward.

Continued moves toward integration seem likely, as well. Recent waves of mergers and acquisitions within the video game industry by Sony and Microsoft risk leaving Nintendo with an ever narrower road to success. Deals like the 10-year agreement with Microsoft suggests the company will continue to be a heavyweight in the industry, but its purchase of its own film production studio seems to suggest a more solid way forward, though one which require the company's culture to adapt (Ralph-Donaldson, 2023; Morris, 2022). Whether this will mean the company needs to expand into other areas of media remains to be seen but is certainly something to consider. That, in turn, might mean changing long-term practices like the company's approach to cash reserves and relatively lean employment. In whatever way the company moves forward, its impact on the games industry and its reach beyond is both clear and profound. What is clear is that the company has been focused on a particular understanding of its products and its audiences, and that focus has shaped its approaches. This has often meant going against the grain of its competitors, valuing itself and its products differently and being willing to take risks other companies haven't. In so doing, the company has both cultivated its power globally, using it carefully to further its own goals.

References

D'Angelo, W. (2023, May 15). The Legend of Zelda: Tears of the Kingdom Sells Nearly 500,000 at Retail in France. *VGChartz*. https://www.vgchartz.com/article/457185/the-legend-of-zelda-tears-of-the-kingdom-sells-nearly-500000-at-retail-in-france/

Dring, C. D. H. of G. (2023, May 14). The Legend of Zelda: Tears of the Kingdom is the Second Biggest Nintendo Launch in UK History. *GamesIndustry.biz*. https://www.gamesindustry.biz/the-legend-of-zelda-tears-of-the-kingdom-shatters-sales-records-in-the-uk-uk-boxed-charts

Friedman, M. (2023, April 27). Super Nintendo World Investments Help Boost Universal Parks Profits. *Inside the Magic*. https://insidethemagic.net/2023/04/super-nintendo-world-investments-help-boost-universal-theme-parks-profits-ed1/

Gould, E. (2023, April 11). *Nintendo Isn't Messing Around Searching for the Zelda: Tears of the Kingdom Leaker*. TechRadar. https://www.techradar.com/news/nintendo-isnt-messing-around-searching-for-the-zelda-tears-of-the-kingdom-leaker

Kelly, S., Klézl, V., Israilidis, J., Malone, N., & Butler, S. (2021). Digital Supply Chain Management in the Videogames Industry: A Systematic Literature Review. *The Computer Games Journal, 10*(1), 19–40.

Kocurek, C. A. (2015). *Coin-Operated Americans: Rebooting Boyhood at the Video Game Arcade*. Minneapolis: University of Minnesota Press.

Lewellyn, A. (2023, May 12). *What to know about Zelda: Tears of the Kingdom. Vox.* https://www.vox.com/culture/2023/5/12/23721846/zelda-tears-of-the-kingdom-today-explained

Litchfield, T. (2023, May 7). Nintendo Seems to Have Fired Back Over the Tears of the Kingdom Leak by DMCAing Popular Switch Emulation Tools. *PC Gamer.* https://www.pcgamer.com/nintendo-seems-to-have-fired-back-over-the-tears-of-the-kingdom-leak-by-dmcaing-popular-switch-emulation-tools/

MacDonald, K. (2023, May 15). 'Is this Really Going to Work?' The Makers of Mega-Hit Video Game the Legend of Zelda: Tears of the Kingdom. *The Guardian.* https://www.theguardian.com/games/2023/may/15/makers-mega-hit-video-game-legend-of-zelda-tears-of-the-kingdom-hyrule

Malhotra, R. (2023, May 14). "The Super Mario Bros. [Movie]" Continues Record Breaking Run at the Global Box Office. *Collider.* https://collider.com/super-mario-bros-movie-global-box-office-1-point-2-billion/

Morris, C. (2022, July 14). *Nintendo Just Bought a Movie Studio – What It Means for the Company.* Fast Company. https://www.fastcompany.com/90769479/nintendo-movie-studio-dynamo-pictures

Mui, T. (2023, May 10). Nintendo President Says New Hardware Isn't Due for at Least a Year Despite Slowing Switch Sales. *The FPS Review.* https://www.thefpsreview.com/2023/05/09/nintendo-president-says-new-hardware-isnt-due-for-at-least-a-year-despite-slowing-switch-sales/

Nichols, R. (2011). Before Play, Production: Contributions of Political Economy to the Field of Game Studies. In *Videogames Studies: Concepts, Cultures, and Communication* (pp. 39–47). Leiden, Netherlands: Brill.

Nichols, R. (2014). *The Video Game Business (International Screen Industries).* New York, NY: Palgrave Macmillan on Behalf of the British Film Institute.

Nichols, R. (2020). Pokémon Go: Globalization. In M. T. Payne & N. B. Huntemann (Eds.), *How to Play Video Games* (pp. 250–258). New York, USA: New York University Press. https://doi.org/10.18574/9781479830404-032

Payne, M. T. (2019). "Now They're Playing with Power!": Nintendo's Classics and Franchise Legacy Management. In J. Fleury, B. Hikari Harzheim, & S. Mamber (Eds.), *The Franchise Era: Managing Media in the Digital Economy* (pp. 105–118). Edinburgh: Edinburgh University Press.

Ralph-Donaldson, T. (2023, February 28). Microsoft Signs 10-Year Contract to Bring Xbox Games to Nintendo – Here's What that Means for Players. *The Conversation.* http://theconversation.com/microsoft-signs-10-year-contract-to-bring-xbox-games-to-nintendo-heres-what-that-means-for-players-200778

Taylor-Hill, G. (2023, May 15). Nintendo Switch Has Made $69 Billion in Seven Years. *Insider Gaming.* https://insider-gaming.com/nintendo-switch-69-billion-revenue/

Tomaselli, F., Luiz, T., Di Serio, L., Luciel, S., & de Oliveira, L. (2008, May 9). *Value Chain Management and Competitive Strategy in the Home Video Game Industry.* POMS 19th Annual Conference, La Jolla, CA. file:///Users/rjnic/Downloads/Value_Chain_Management_and_Competitive_Strategy_in.pdf

Index

Note: Page numbers in *italics* indicate a figure and page numbers in **bold** indicate a table on the corresponding page.

For Product Safety Concerns and Information please contact our EU
representative GPSR@taylorandfrancis.com
Taylor & Francis Verlag GmbH, Kaufingerstraße 24, 80331 München, Germany

www.ingramcontent.com/pod-product-compliance
Lightning Source LLC
Chambersburg PA
CBHW061833220326
41599CB00027B/5265

9 780367 776404